Negotiate Like Your Life Depends On It

23 Tricks to Close a Deal Like a Ninja

Julian Tansley

Journey Together LTD

Contents

Introduction

Let's be real—negotiation sounds about as fun as a root canal. When most people think of negotiating, they see high-stakes boardroom conflicts, dramatic court skirmishes, or perhaps a car salesman in a cheap suit trying to upsell them on rust protection. It's no surprise that many of us would prefer to avoid the whole process completely.

But here's the thing: whether you realize it or not, you've been negotiating your entire life. Remember when you were a kid and you convinced your parents to let you stay up an extra hour past bedtime? Negotiation. Or when you sweet-talked your way out of that speeding ticket in college? Negotiation. Heck, even deciding where to order takeout with your significant other involves some level of back-and-forth (extra points if you can get them to agree to Thai food for the third night in a row).

Negotiating Your Way Through Life (Without Losing Your Cool)

The point is that negotiating isn't limited to bigwig CEOs or high-powered attorneys. It is an essential life skill that touches almost every part of our everyday lives. However, most of us have never been taught how to do it effectively. We struggle through these exchanges, frequently feeling embarrassed, anxious, or just frustrated. We second-guess ourselves, kick ourselves for not speaking up, or, worse, consent to something we don't want just to avoid rocking the boat.

Sound familiar? If so, you're definitely not alone. In fact, I'd argue that the vast majority of people struggle with negotiation on some level:

- Perhaps you fear confrontation, so you simply smile and nod, even if you strongly disagree.

- Perhaps you're a people-pleaser who despises the idea of disappointing others, so you overwork yourself to the point of burnout.

- Or perhaps you are simply terrified of the entire procedure, fearing that you will say the wrong thing or appear silly in front of your boss/client/coworkers.

I get it. Believe me, I've been in that situation too. I used to call myself a "reformed pushover," and for years, I avoided anything that felt like a negotiation. I would take the first salary offer that came my way, let clients take advantage of me, and cross my fingers that being nice would lead to good things for me.

I only understood the importance of negotiation skills when I launched my own business. Suddenly, I was responsible for everything—establishing my prices, handling demanding clients, and persuading investors to trust my brilliant idea. Honestly, it turned out to be a significant learning curve. I made mistakes. My feelings took a hit. I've missed out on more offers than I want to admit. But, you know what? I learned a lot from it all. I've grown up. And gradually, I became quite skilled at this entire bargaining process.

★★★

Why This Book Is Your Secret Weapon

That's why I'm writing this book. Not because I'm some infallible negotiation guru (trust me, I still have plenty of facepalm moments), but because I've been where you are. I know how daunting it can feel to put yourself out there, to advocate for what you want, to risk hearing that dreaded word: "No." But I also know firsthand how transformative mastering the art of negotiation can be—not just for your career, but for your entire life.

Think about it. What would it mean for you to:

- Walk into your boss's office with confidence and ask for that well-deserved increase.

- Finally, have that difficult chat with a problematic employee. Are you confident that you can manage any pushback?

- Stand firm on your pricing with a demanding client, confident you're worth every penny.

The bottom line is this: negotiation is a muscle. And like any muscle, it gets stronger with practice. The more you flex it, the more comfortable you'll become with the process. The more you put yourself out there, the easier it will be to hold your own in any situation. And the more you learn about the psychology and the tactics behind effective negotiation, the better equipped you'll be to advocate for yourself and what you deserve.

And that, my friend, is where this book comes in. It is your own negotiation boot camp, complete with step-by-step strategies, real-world examples, and a little tough love to keep you focused. We'll discuss everything from the fundamentals of preparation and research to the psychology of persuasion, the art of active listening, and how to handle difficult situations such as cultural differences.

But be warned: this isn't your average dry, dull business book. We're going to have fun as we go along. We'll have some laughs, maybe cringe a bit, and perhaps even get teary-eyed (mainly from the jokes, but you know how negotiations are). So, let me tell you a little secret: learning to bargain may actually be rather pleasurable. Honestly, it can be really exciting—once you get over the first anxieties and realize how much influence you have over your destiny.

So whether you're an entrepreneur looking to close more deals, a freelancer tired of getting lowballed, or just someone who wants to hold their own in any conversation, this book is for you. By the time we're done, you'll be armed with a veritable arsenal of negotiation tricks, hacks, and ninja-level mind games (okay, maybe not mind games—that sounds a little too evil villainy). But more importantly, you'll have the confidence to put them into action, stand up for what you want, and never settle for less than you're worth.

So, are you ready to become a true bargaining ninja? Great. Let us do this. But first, a brief disclaimer. This book may or may not turn you into a ninja. But it will improve your ability to advocate for yourself, your ideas, and your worth. It will teach you to handle even the most difficult negotiations with grace, poise, and a wicked sense of fun. And it might just transform your life.

At the very least, it'll make for some seriously impressive cocktail party chatter.

So grab a snack (pro tip: negotiation is always easier on a full stomach), get comfortable, and let's dive in. Your inner negotiation ninja awaits.

Chapter One

Mastering the Mindset of a Negotiation Ninja

Let us begin the journey to transform your negotiation skills from basic to ninja-level mastery. This chapter is about more than just absorbing information; it is about reinventing your attitude to negotiation, making you knowledgeable and incredibly effective in any negotiating circumstance.

How to Channel Your Inner Batman

Picture this: you're just about to step into the biggest negotiation of your life. It's a big deal, and you might feel a bit jittery, just like a kid getting ready to go on stage for their first school play. What do you do? Simple. You channel your inner Batman.

Now, I know what you're thinking. "But I don't have a billion-dollar fortune, a fancy Batmobile, or a utility belt packed with gadgets!" You know what? You don't need any of that. You really just need to have the right mindset.

You see, Batman isn't just your typical superhero; he's actually a really skilled negotiator. Just take a moment to consider it. He often faces off against some of the most dangerous criminals in Gotham, relying solely on his wits, skills, and a strong sense of confidence. And that, my friend, is what makes a difference in negotiation success.

The Power of Confidence

Confidence is the foundation of effective negotiation. When you project confidence, you convey a strong message to your counterpart: "I know my worth, I believe in my position, and I'm not going to back down easily." This establishes the tone for the entire interaction and may frequently tilt the scales in your favor before you even begin negotiating terms.

But what if you need more confidence? What if the thought of negotiating makes your palms sweat and your stomach turn? Do not worry, even Batman had to start somewhere. Here are some strategies to help you increase your negotiation confidence:

- **Visualize success**: Before walking into a negotiation, take a few minutes to close your eyes and envision the outcome you want. Imagine yourself delivering a compelling case, efficiently managing objections, and eventually achieving a favorable agreement. By mentally rehearsing your success, you prepare your brain to make it a reality.

- **Strike a power pose**: This might sound a little silly, but bear with me. According to research, taking a forceful stance for just two minutes, with your spine straightened, shoulders back, and hands on your hips, can greatly enhance your confidence. So before your next big negotiation, find a private spot, channel your inner superhero, and let your body language work its magic.

- **Reframe self-doub**t: Even the most seasoned negotiators sometimes fall victim to imposter syndrome - that nagging feeling that you're not good enough, smart enough, or experienced enough to succeed. When negative thoughts arise, attempt to reframe things more positively. Instead of saying, "I'm not ready for this," tell yourself, "I've thoroughly prepared and am excited to put my skills to the test." Over time, this type of self-talk might help you silence your inner critic and gain confidence.

Unleashing Your Inner Superhero

At the end of the day, channeling your inner Batman is all about mindset. It's about walking into every negotiation with the unshakable belief that you have something valuable to offer and that you're worthy of respect and consideration.

Will you always get everything you want? Of course not. Even Batman takes a few punches now and then. But by approaching each interaction with confidence, poise, and a touch of superhero swagger, you'll be amazed at how much more effective and enjoyable negotiating can be.

So the next time you feel nervous before a big negotiation, take a deep breath, straighten your cape (okay, your standard work attire will also suffice), and remember: you don't need a bat signal to be a negotiation hero. You just need to believe in yourself and let your inner Batman shine.

✷✷✷

Embracing a Growth Mindset Because Even Ninjas Need to Learn New Tricks

Picture a ninja in action. They're nimble, adaptable, and always ready to face new challenges head-on. Now imagine that ninja suddenly decides, "You know what? I'm good. I have studied enough. It's time to hang up my nunchucks and call it a day. Isn't it almost comical? Because we all know that true ninjas are constantly learning, growing, and improving.

The same idea applies to negotiations. No matter how skilled or experienced you are, there is always room to learn, adapt, and improve your skills. And that, my friend, is where embracing a growth mindset comes in.

Fixed vs. Growth: A Tale of Two Mindsets

Stanford psychologist Carol Dweck developed the concept of fixed vs. development mindsets in her seminal book "Mindset: The New Psychology of Success." People with a fixed mindset believe that their abilities are static and unchangeable. For example, you're either born a great negotiator or not. On the other hand, those with a growth mindset regard skills as flexible and adaptable to effort; being a master negotiator is something that anyone can do with practice and commitment.

As you might guess, adopting a growth mindset is crucial for long-term success in negotiation (and in life). When you view challenges as opportunities to learn rather than threats to your ego, you open yourself up to a world of possibility and potential.

Cultivating a Growth Mindset

So how can you shift from a fixed to a growth mindset? Here are a few strategies to try:

- **Reframe challenges as opportunities**: The next time you face a tough negotiation or encounter a skill gap, resist the urge to get discouraged. Instead, view it as a chance to stretch yourself and expand your abilities. Embrace the discomfort as a sign that you're growing.

- **Celebrate small wins**: Negotiation mastery is a journey, not a destination. Take time to acknowledge and celebrate your progress, no matter how incremental. Did you successfully use a new technique in your last negotiation? High five! Did you bounce back from a tough objection with grace and poise? Victory dance! These small wins add up over time and help fuel your motivation to keep learning and improving.

- **Seek feedback and use it constructively**: One of the hallmarks of a growth mindset is a willingness to seek out and learn from feedback - even when it's not always positive. After each negotiation, take a few minutes to reflect on what went well and where you could improve. If possible, ask your counterpart or a trusted colleague for their honest input. Then, use that feedback as a roadmap for your continued growth and development.

Embracing the Journey

Even the most skilled negotiators started as beginners. They fumbled, made mistakes, and most likely had some cringe-worthy moments along the way. However, they continued to practice, learn, and improve, finally distinguishing themselves.

Adopting a growth mindset in negotiation means embracing the journey rather than fixating on the destination. It entails being open to trying new approaches, even if they feel awkward at first. It also entails viewing failure as a necessary stepping stone toward success rather than a setback.

And here's the best part: when you approach negotiation with a growth mindset, you relieve the pressure to be perfect. You give yourself permission to be a work in progress—to make mistakes, learn from them, and come back stronger and savvier than before.

So the next time you think, "I'm just not cut out for this negotiation thing," remember that even the greatest ninjas began somewhere. Embrace the adventure, keep learning, and believe that with time and experience, you can negotiate like a pro.

***

How to Read People Like a Psychic

Imagine walking into a negotiation and immediately seeing that the person across from you looks stressed, anxious, and uncertain about your proposal. You may not have a crystal ball or the power to read minds, but you have something just as powerful: emotional intelligence.

Emotional intelligence, or EQ for short, is all about controlling and managing your feelings while also being aware of what others are experiencing. It's like having a secret decoder that lets you understand how people act, and it really changes the game when you're negotiating.

The Role of EQ in Negotiation

Think about it: negotiations are simply high-stakes interactions between individuals. And where there are people, there are emotions - fear, excitement, anger, hope, disappointment. These emotions swirl beneath the surface of every negotiation, impacting how individuals think, communicate, and make decisions.

As a negotiator, you should focus on more than just the logical arguments and factual evidence presented. You must also be intensely aware of the emotional undercurrents at play and use that knowledge to guide your approach.

Sharpening Your EQ Skills

So how can you boost your emotional intelligence and start reading people like a modern-day Sherlock Holmes? Here are a few practical tips:

- **Practice active listening**: Pay close attention to what your counterpart says and how they say it. What's their tone of voice? Are they speaking quickly or slowly? Do they seem excited, anxious, or frustrated? You'll gain valuable insight into their emotional state by tuning into these subtle cues.

- **Observe nonverbal cues**: A whopping 70-93% of

communication is nonverbal, which means if you're only focusing on the words spoken, you're missing a huge piece of the puzzle. During negotiations, watch for telltale body language signs like crossed arms (defensiveness), fidgeting (nervousness), or leaning forward (engagement). These cues can speak volumes about how your counterpart is really feeling.

- **Manage your own emotions**: Emotional intelligence isn't just about reading others; it's also about being aware of and in control of your own emotions. When tensions run high in a negotiation, it's all too easy to get swept up in the heat of the moment and let your feelings dictate your response. You can keep your cool and make more rational, strategic decisions by practicing techniques like deep breathing, mentally reframing the situation, or even calling for a short break when needed.

Putting It into Practice

Let's say you're negotiating a big contract with a new client. As you're discussing pricing, you notice that your counterpart starts to fidget in their seat and their tone becomes a bit clipped. An emotionally intelligent response might look like this:

"I'm sensing some hesitation around the pricing structure. Is there a specific concern you have that we still need to address? I want to make sure we're on the same page and can find a solution that works for both of us."

Acknowledging their pain and allowing them to share more demonstrates empathy, establishes trust, and may unearth vital facts that will help you achieve a mutually beneficial agreement.

The Bottom Line

The ability to read people and situations is an extremely essential talent in both negotiations and everyday life. The good news is that it is a talent everyone can learn with practice.

By improving your active listening skills, paying attention to nonverbal signs, and controlling your own emotional responses, you'll begin to see things you didn't previously. This is like having a hidden window into what makes people tick, and that information may be a wonderful tool for developing highly effective bargaining methods.

So, the next time you're in a negotiation, tap into your inner psychic. Tune in to emotional cues, trust your instincts, and utilize that knowledge to establish stronger, more productive relationships. With some practice (and perhaps a crystal ball for good measure), you'll read people like a pro in no time.

$$***$$

Reframing Failure as Feedback (A Jedi Mind Trick)

As Yoda once said, "Failure is the greatest teacher." Now I understand what you are thinking. "That's easy for you to say, you little green sage!" You can spend your days meditating in a swamp while I'm out here negotiating with clients that make Darth Vader look like a teddy bear.

But here's the thing: Yoda was onto something. Failure isn't just an inevitable part of the negotiation process; it's an essential one. Every misstep, setback, and deal that doesn't quite go according to plan are powerful opportunities for growth and learning. The key is how you choose to frame them.

The Negotiator's Path

Imagine if Luke Skywalker had given up the first time he failed to levitate a rock with his mind. Or if he'd thrown in the towel after getting his hand chopped off by dear old dad. The Star Wars saga would have been a whole lot shorter (and a lot less interesting).

The same principle applies to your journey as a negotiator. You will confront challenges. You'll make errors. You will have moments when you wonder if you're cut out for this "Jedi mind trick" stuff. However, if you can learn to see those mistakes as feedback, as vital data points on your road to mastery, you will be unstoppable.

Strategies for Reframing Failure

So how do you make this mental shift? How do you go from seeing failure as a personal affront to viewing it as a powerful teacher? Here are a few Jedi-approved strategies:

- **Conduct a post-negotiation debrief**: After every negotiation (successful or not), take some time to reflect on what happened. What went well? What could you have done differently? What did you learn about your counterpart, the situation, or yourself? By approaching the experience with curiosity rather than judgment, you'll see valuable lessons in even the most challenging interactions.

- **Embrace the "not yet" mentality**: When you think, "I'm just not good at this," add one crucial word: "yet." Remind yourself that negotiation is a skill like any other—one that can be developed and refined over time. No one starts as a master, and even the most seasoned negotiators are constantly learning and growing.

- **Aim for progress, not perfection**: Perfectionism is the enemy of growth. If you go into every negotiation expecting to nail it flawlessly, you'll be setting yourself up for disappointment (and a whole lot of self-doubt). Instead, focus on making small, incremental improvements. Celebrate the little victories and use the missteps as fuel for your next attempt.

The Power of Persistence

History is full of examples of great negotiators who failed before they succeeded. Take Benjamin Franklin: before he was brokering deals on the world stage, he was getting kicked out of England for stirring up political trouble. Or consider Nelson Mandela, who spent 27 years in prison before leading South Africa through a historic negotiation process and becoming the country's first Black president.

The common thread between these stories? Persistence. A willingness to learn from failure, dust themselves off, and try again. A belief that setbacks are just pit stops on the road to success.

Negotiation is a bit like mastering the ways of the Jedi—it's a journey that lasts a lifetime. There will be ups and downs, wins and setbacks. If you can tackle each experience with a growth mindset—seeing failure as just feedback and using it to drive your progress—you'll be on the right path to becoming great at negotiation.

Next time you're in a negotiation that doesn't go as you hoped, just think of Yoda. Just take a moment to breathe, think about what you've learned, and remember that every setback is just a part of the journey to success.

So, what if things don't go as planned? Just whip out a lightsaber. That does the job!

Just a heads-up: bringing a lightsaber to negotiations is probably not a smart idea. I've heard it's not a good idea and it violates workplace safety rules.

Wrapping Up

Mastering the mindset of a negotiation ninja isn't about being the smartest, the toughest, or the most unflappable person in the room. It's about developing a mental framework that allows you to approach each interaction with confidence, adaptability, and a hunger for continuous growth.

By channeling your inner Batman and projecting self-assurance, embracing a growth mindset and viewing challenges as opportunities, sharpening your emotional intelligence skills to read people like a pro, and reframing failures as valuable feedback, you'll be well on your way to negotiation mastery.

But remember: this is just the beginning. The path to becoming a true negotiation ninja is one of lifelong learning, experimentation, and improvement. Embrace the journey, stay open to new ideas and approaches, and never stop striving to improve.

"You must have patience, my young Padawan," as a Yoda-like negotiation guru might say. Building a ninja mindset is all about taking your time, practicing, and thinking about yourself along the way. With a little persistence and a mindset for growth, you'll be tapping into your inner superhero and making deals like a Jedi master before you know it.

So go forth, my aspiring negotiation ninjas. May the force (and a healthy dose of emotional intelligence) be with you.

Chapter Two

Preparing for Battle: Research and Strategy

Ever heard the saying, "Victory loves preparation"? Well, negotiation is no different. In this chapter, you'll learn how to dig deep, plan smart, and walk into any negotiation armed with all the information and strategy you need to win. After all, even the best ninjas only leap into action with a plan.

How to Be a Detective in a Business Suit

Picture this: you're about to walk into the most important negotiation of your career. The stakes are high, the pressure is on, and you feel about as prepared as a kid cramming for a pop quiz. What do you do? Simple. You channel your inner Sherlock Holmes (minus the pipe and funny hat).

You see, careful research is at the heart of every successful negotiation. It's all about knowing your stuff, predicting your counterpart's next move, and approaching the situation strategically. In other words, it's like being a detective dressed in a business suit.

Why Research Matters

Think about it: would you walk into a courtroom without building a case? Would you perform surgery without studying the patient's medical history? Of course not. So why would you walk into a negotiation without doing your due diligence?

Here's the thing: knowledge equals power. The more you know about your counterpart, the market, and the circumstances surrounding your negotiation, the more prepared you will be to fight for your interests and discover mutually beneficial solutions.

Key Elements to Research

So what exactly should you be researching? Here are a few key areas to focus on:

1. Your Counterpart's Needs, Goals, and Motivations

   - What are they hoping to achieve through this negotiation?

   - What pain points or challenges are they trying to address?

   - What do they value most (e.g., price, quality, timeline)?

2. The Market, Industry Standards, and Relevant Data

   - What are your industry's typical price points, contract terms, or service level agreements?

   - What are the latest trends, disruptions, or innovations shaping the market?

   - What benchmarks or case studies can you reference to support your position?

3. Past Negotiation Patterns or Preferences

   - How has your counterpart approached similar negotiations in the past?

   - What concessions or compromises have they made (or refused to make)?

- What communication or decision-making style do they tend to favor?

Tools and Techniques for Gathering Intel

Now that you know what to research, let's talk about how to do it. Here are a few ninja-approved tools and techniques:

1. Online Research

- Scour company websites, press releases, and social media accounts for insights

- Dive into industry reports, trade publications, and market analyses

- Use LinkedIn to learn more about your counterpart's background, connections, and interests

2. Leveraging Your Network

- Reach out to colleagues, mentors, or friends who may have worked with your counterpart in the past

- Attend industry events, conferences, or networking sessions to gather intel and build relationships

- Join online forums, groups, or communities where your counterpart's peers or customers congregate

3. Asking Subtle Pre-Negotiation Questions

- When setting up the negotiation, ask casual questions to gauge their priorities or constraints (e.g., "Just to make sure we make the most of our time together, what are the key issues you're hoping to address?")

- During small talk or rapport-building, listen for clues about their interests, motivations, or decision-making process

- If appropriate, consider sending a brief pre-negotiation questionnaire or agenda to gather input and align expectations

Putting It All Together

By now, you might be thinking: "Whoa, that's a lot of research! How am I supposed to find the time for all that?"

Fair point. Conducting extensive research requires effort, but believe me, it is worthwhile. And with some practice, it will seem like second nature.

Think of it like being Sherlock Holmes but with spreadsheets and Google searches instead of a magnifying glass and a deerstalker hat. You're gathering clues, piecing together the puzzle, and building a case to help you crack the negotiation code.

And you know what's great? The more you learn, the more confident you'll be when you step into that negotiation room. You'll get a better idea of what you want, what's doable, and how to make it happen. You'll be ready to tackle objections, come up with persuasive points, and discover creative solutions that make everyone feel like a winner.

So go forth, my dear Watson. Put on your detective hat (or business suit), do your homework, and get ready to solve the mystery of successful negotiation.

***

Identifying Key Stakeholders and Decision-Makers and Knowing When to Send in the Charm Offensive

Okay, you've done your research. You've got a wealth of information that would make Sherlock Holmes pleased. But, before you rush into that bargaining room with guns (or spreadsheets) blazing, there's one more critical step: determining who the main players are and how to win them over.

Why Knowing the Key Players is Critical

Imagine this: you spend weeks preparing the perfect pitch, only to realize you've been negotiating with the wrong person the whole time. Awkward, right?

That's why it's so important to identify the key stakeholders and decision-makers. Targeting the right people from the start can save you time, energy, and potential embarrassment.

How to Identify Decision-Makers

So how do you figure out who's who in the negotiation zoo? Here are a few clues to look for:

1. Organizational Hierarchies and Job Titles

   ○ Look for roles like CEO, CFO, VP, or Director - these folks typically have the authority to make big decisions

   ○ Pay attention to who reports to whom and who seems to have the most influence within the organization

2. Clues from Past Interactions or Meeting Dynamics

   ○ Notice who does most of the talking, asks the tough questions, or seems to command the room

   ○ Look for deference or approval-seeking behaviors from other team members

   ○ If you've had prior negotiations with this company, reflect on who seemed to have the final say

Strategies for Influencing Stakeholders

Once you've identified the key players, it's time to start thinking about how to get them on your side. Here are a few strategies to try:

1. Building Rapport with Gatekeepers

   - Gatekeepers are the people who control access to the decision-makers - think executive assistants, receptionists, or project managers

   - Treat them with respect, build a friendly relationship, and they may just become your biggest advocates

2. Crafting Messages that Resonate with Different Levels of Authority

   - When communicating with executives, focus on big-picture strategy, ROI, and competitive advantage

   - When talking to middle managers, emphasize how your proposal will make their job easier, improve their metrics, or enhance their team's performance

   - When interacting with individual contributors, highlight the personal benefits they'll experience, like increased efficiency, better tools, or more opportunities for growth

Tactics for Delivering a Charm Offensive

So, I can guess what's on your mind: "Charm offensive?" Isn't that just a clever way of putting it as manipulation?

Not really. A charm offensive is about connecting with people, discovering shared interests, and fostering a friendly, cooperative atmosphere while keeping your goals and values in mind.

Here are a few tips for delivering a charm offensive that feels authentic, not icky:

1. Mirroring Communication Styles

   - If your counterpart is formal and analytical, adjust your language and tone to match

   - If they're more casual and conversational, loosen up a bit and let your personality shine through

   - The goal is to make them feel comfortable and understood, not to be a chameleon

2. Subtle Flattery and Personalized Touches

   - Do your research (see previous section) and find something genuine to compliment - their company's recent success, their thought leadership in the industry, or even their alma mater

   - Add personal touches to your communications, like referencing a shared interest or following up on a topic they mentioned in passing

   - The key is to be sincere, not sycophantic - people can sniff out fake flattery from a mile away

Let's look at an example of the charm offensive done right:

Scenario: You're negotiating a partnership deal with a tech startup. The CEO is known for being tough and no-nonsense, but you've heard through the grapevine that she's passionate about mentoring young entrepreneurs.

Approach:

- Before the negotiation, you should contact the CEO's assistant and ask if you can do anything to make the meeting more productive or efficient. You can also mention that you're impressed by the CEO's commitment to giving back to the startup community.

- During the negotiation, you should come prepared with data and case studies that speak directly to the CEO's priorities. You should also ask about their experience as a mentor and share a brief anecdote about a young entrepreneur you've recently advised.

- In your follow-up email, based on your conversation, you include a link to an article you thought the CEO might find interesting. You also reiterate your shared goal of supporting the next generation of innovators.

See what happened there? You put in the effort, found genuine ways to connect, and showed that you care about more than just your own interests - you're all about the bigger picture.

That's how you pull off a charm offensive without coming across like a used car salesman, my friend.

The Bottom Line

Figuring out who the key stakeholders and decision-makers are is crucial in any negotiation. It ensures that you're targeting the right people, crafting the right messages, and building the right relationships.

And when it comes to influencing those key players, a bit of charm can make a difference. Just keep it real, stay relevant, and focus on your goals.

After all, you're not just a ninja - you're a negotiation ninja with a heart of gold.

***

Anticipating Objections and Counterarguments Because You're Not Just a Ninja, You're a Mind Reader

Pop quiz: what's the one thing that can derail even the most well-prepared negotiation?

If you said "unexpected objections," give yourself a gold star (and maybe a cookie).

The truth is, no matter how brilliant your proposal or how charm-offensive your smile is, you're bound to face some pushback. The key is to anticipate those objections before they're even raised - and have a plan for how to counter them.

In other words, you need to be a ninja and a mind reader.

Why Anticipating Objections Makes You Look Prepared and Confident

Picture this: you're in the middle of a negotiation, and your counterpart hits you with an objection you never saw coming. You freeze, you stutter, you start to sweat. Not exactly the picture of confidence, right?

Now imagine the same scenario, but this time, you've got a response ready to go. You calmly address their concern, offer a solution, and keep the conversation moving forward—boom - instant credibility.

Thinking ahead about objections shows you've put in the effort, you get where the other person is coming from, and you're all set to work through any issues together. It shows that you're not just making it up as you go along - you're someone who knows their stuff and has considered every detail.

Common Objections and How to Counter Them

So what are some of the most common objections you might face? Here are a few examples:

1. Price Concerns

- Objection: "Your price is too high," "We don't have the budget," or "Your competitor is cheaper."

- Countermove: Demonstrate your unique value, highlight the long-term ROI or cost savings, or propose a creative pricing structure (e.g., phased payments or volume discounts).

2. Timing Issues

- Objection: "We're not ready to make a decision," "We need more time," or "Let's revisit this next quarter."

- Countermove: To create a sense of urgency, highlight the cost of inaction, offer a low-risk trial or pilot program, or propose a phased implementation timeline.

3. Skepticism About Your Offer

- Objection: "I'm not sure this will work for us," "We've tried something like this before and it failed," or "What makes you different from everyone else?"

- Countermove: Provide concrete proof of your capabilities (e.g., case studies, testimonials, data), address their specific concerns head-on, and emphasize your unique differentiators or value proposition.

Techniques for Predicting Objections

Now, you might be thinking: "That's all well and good, but how do I predict what objections they'll raise?"

Fair question. Here are a few techniques to try:

1. Put Yourself in Their Shoes

- Imagine you're on the other side of the negotiation table.

What concerns, doubts, or reservations would you have?

- Consider their role, their goals, and their potential risks or challenges. What might hold them back from saying yes?

2. Review Past Negotiations or Industry Trends

- Look for patterns or common objections that have come up in similar negotiations or deals

- Stay up-to-date on industry news, competitor moves, or market shifts that could influence your counterpart's perspective

3. Ask Probing Questions During the Negotiation

- As you're discussing your proposal, listen for hints or clues about potential objections

- Ask open-ended questions to uncover their hesitations or concerns (e.g., "What are your thoughts on this so far?" or "Is there anything else you'd like to know before we move forward?")

Methods for Preparing Counterarguments

Alright, you've predicted the objections - now what? It's time to craft your counterarguments. Here's how:

1. Use Data and Facts to Back Up Your Points

- Gather evidence, statistics, or case studies that support your position

- Use specific numbers or examples to make your case more compelling

2. Craft Empathetic Responses to Diffuse Resistance

- Acknowledge their concerns and show that you understand

where they're coming from

- Use phrases like "I hear you," "That's a valid point," or "I can see how that might be a concern"

- Reframe the objection as an opportunity to find a mutually beneficial solution

And remember, it's not just what you say - it's how you say it. Use confident body language, maintain eye contact, and keep your tone calm and collaborative.

Mind Reading 101

By now, you might feel like a regular Professor X (minus the shiny bald head and mutant powers). But here's the thing: you don't need to be a literal mind reader to anticipate objections.

You just need to be a diligent researcher, an active listener, and a creative problem-solver. You need to put yourself in your counterpart's shoes, look for patterns and clues, and practice the art of empathy.

And most importantly? You need to remember that objections aren't roadblocks - they're opportunities. They're a chance to deepen your understanding, strengthen your relationship, and find a solution that works for everyone.

So go forth, my ninja apprentice. Sharpen your mind-reading skills, hone your counterarguments, and get ready to turn objections into victories.

Because with a little preparation and a lot of practice, you'll be negotiating like a true psychic in no time.

✶✶✶

How to Make Them an Offer They Can't Refuse

Picture this: you're sitting across the table from your counterpart, ready to make your pitch. You've done your research, anticipated their objections, and got a few clever persuasion techniques up your sleeve. But as you start to outline your proposal, you see their eyes glaze over. They're nodding politely, but you can tell they're not really sold.

What's going on here? Chances are, you're focusing on the wrong thing. You're probably rattling off a list of features and specifications, hoping that something will stick. But here's the truth: people don't buy features - they buy benefits. They don't care about what your product or service does; they care about what it does for them.

The Power of a Strong Value Proposition

This is where the art of the value proposition comes in. A value proposition is a clear, concise statement that communicates the tangible benefits of your offer. It's not about you or your company; it's about them and their needs.

Crafting a strong value proposition is the secret sauce of negotiation. It's what takes your offer from a bland, forgettable pitch to an irresistible deal that they simply can't refuse.

The Anatomy of an Irresistible Offer

So, what makes a value proposition genuinely compelling? Here are a few key ingredients:

- **Clarity**: Your value prop should be easy to understand and articulate. Avoid jargon, buzzwords, or complex technical terms. Keep it simple, stupid.

- **Relevance**: Your offer should address your counterpart's specific needs, challenges, and objectives. Generic promises will not cut it; you need to show that you understand their unique situation.

- **Tangible Benefits**: Don't just talk about what your offer does; focus on what it achieves. Will it save them time, money, or headaches? Will it make their life easier, their business more profitable, or their team more productive? Paint a vivid picture of the value they'll receive.

- **Proof Points**: It's not enough to make bold claims - you need to back them up with evidence. Use case studies, testimonials, or data to demonstrate that you've delivered similar results for others. Make it real and relatable.

Tailoring Your Pitch

Of course, a one-size-fits-all value proposition rarely lands. To make your offer irresistible, you need to tailor it to your specific audience.

Start by putting yourself in their shoes. What are their top priorities and pain points? What do they value most? What's keeping them up at night? The more you can align your offer with their deepest needs and desires, the more persuasive it will be.

Next, consider their communication style and preferences. Are they data-driven and analytical? Focus on hard numbers and ROI. Are they more relationship-oriented? Emphasize the personal benefits and emotional appeal. Are they pressed for time? Keep it concise and to the point.

Bringing It All Together

Now, let's see this in action. Suppose you're a software vendor trying to sell a new CRM system to a mid-sized company. A generic value prop might sound something like this:

"Our software streamlines your sales process and improves efficiency."

Not bad, but not exactly irresistible. Now, let's see what happens when we put our value proposition formula to work:

"Imagine closing 25% more deals without working longer hours or chasing dead-end leads. That's the power of our CRM system. We've helped businesses like yours boost revenue by an average of $500K in the first year alone while saving your sales reps up to 10 hours per week on administrative tasks. It's not just a software upgrade - it's a game-changer for your bottom line, your team's productivity, and your peace of mind. So, what would you do with an extra half a million dollars and a team that's firing on all cylinders?"

See the difference? By focusing on clear, relevant, and tangible benefits, backing them up with proof points, and tailoring the message to the audience, we've transformed a forgettable pitch into an offer they can't refuse.

The Godfather Principle

Now, I know what you're thinking. "This all sounds great, but what if they still say no? What if they're just not interested?"

Well, that's where the Godfather Principle comes in. In the immortal words of Don Corleone, "I'm gonna make him an offer he can't refuse."

No, I'm not suggesting you threaten your counterpart with violence or blackmail (although that would make for a much more exciting negotiation). The point is this: if you've done your research, identified their deepest needs and desires, and crafted a value proposition that speaks directly to those needs, you've already made them an offer they can't refuse.

Sure, they might try to haggle on price or push back on certain terms. But if you've tapped into the core of what they truly want and need, you've got the upper hand. You've made yourself essential, indispensable, irresistible.

So, as you're crafting your next pitch, channel your inner Godfather. Make them an offer that's so perfectly tailored, so irresistibly valuable, that they simply can't walk away.

And if all else fails? Well, there's always the horse head in the bed trick. (Disclaimer: please don't actually put a horse head in anyone's bed. That's frowned upon in most negotiation circles).

In all seriousness, making an irresistible offer is the culmination of all your hard work and preparation. It's the moment when you showcase the full power of your negotiation skills - your research, strategic thinking, persuasive language, and unwavering focus on value.

So go forth and make them an offer they can't refuse. And remember, if you get stuck, just ask yourself: "What would the Godfather do?"

Chapter Three

The Art of Active Listening

What if you could decode what someone is really saying---even when they're not saying it? Active listening is the ultimate negotiation superpower, allowing you to easily understand, connect, and influence. In this chapter, you'll learn to become the human equivalent of a lie detector, a relationship builder, and a mind reader, all rolled into one.

How to Be a Human Lie Detector

Picture this: you're negotiating, and the other party says, "Your offer is very interesting." Do they mean:

A) They're genuinely intrigued and want to learn more

B) They're politely stalling while they come up with an excuse to say no

C) They're being sarcastic, and your offer is actually terrible

The truth is, it could be any of the above. That's why reading between the lines is a critical skill for any negotiation ninja.

Verbal Cues to Watch For:

- Hesitation or hedging language ("maybe," "potentially," "I'll have to think about it")

- Overly formal or vague responses ("That's an interesting

perspective," "Let me get back to you on that")

- Inconsistencies between what they say and how they say it (enthusiastic words with a flat tone)

Nonverbal Cues to Pay Attention To:

- Lack of eye contact or shifty gaze

- Closed body language (crossed arms, turning away)

- Fidgeting or nervous gestures

Now, here's the catch: none of these cues on their own is a surefire sign of deception. Some people are naturally hesitant or fidgety, even when they're telling the truth.

The key is to look for clusters of cues and patterns over time. If someone consistently avoids eye contact, hedges their responses, and has closed body language, there's a good chance they're not being fully honest.

But don't just rely on your intuition. The most effective human lie detectors use active listening to get to the truth.

Active Listening Techniques:

- Ask open-ended questions that encourage elaboration

- Paraphrase what you've heard to confirm your understanding

- Use silence strategically to give them space to fill in the gaps

If you pay attention and actively listen, you'll be able to read between the lines like a pro - and use that insight to navigate the negotiation with confidence.

Think of it like being Sherlock Holmes, but instead of a magnifying glass, your tool is a well-timed "tell me more." Or like being a human polygraph, but instead of measuring heart rate, you're tuning into micro-expressions and tone of voice.

The point is, in negotiation, the truth isn't always in the words being said - it's in the way they're said, the body language that accompanies them, and the pieces left unspoken. By sharpening your lie detection skills, you'll be able to spot incongruences, dig deeper, and get to the heart of what matters to your counterpart.

But remember, with great power comes great responsibility. Use your human lie detector abilities for good—to build trust, find common ground, and create win-win solutions, not to manipulate, intimidate, or deceive.

After all, the goal isn't just to be a human lie detector but a human truth seeker. And the ultimate truth in any negotiation is that everyone wants to feel heard, understood, and valued.

So go forth and detect lies, but more importantly, use your active listening superpowers to uncover the deeper truths that will help you build strong, authentic relationships - in negotiation and in life.

***

Asking Powerful Questions Because Sometimes the Answer Lies in the Question Itself

Have you ever left a conversation feeling like you learned nothing new? Like you were just waiting for your turn to speak instead of truly listening?

If so, you're not alone. In negotiations (and in life), we often focus more on being heard than hearing others. But here's the secret: the most powerful tool in your negotiation arsenal isn't your ability to talk - it's your ability to ask questions.

Why Questions Matter:

- They show genuine interest and curiosity

- They encourage the other party to share more information

- They help you uncover hidden needs, concerns, and motivations

- They give you time to think and regroup while the other party is talking

But not all questions are created equal. To truly harness the power of curiosity, you need to ask the right questions in the right way.

Types of Questions to Ask:

- Open-ended questions that cannot be answered simply with "yes" or "no"

- Clarifying questions that ensure you understand their perspective

- Probing questions that dig deeper into their needs and motivations

- Hypothetical questions that explore potential solutions or scenarios

Examples of Powerful Questions:

- "Can you tell me more about why that's important to you?"

- "What would success look like for you in this negotiation?"

- "If we could find a way to address [concern], what would that mean for you and your team?"

- "Let's say we were able to [proposed solution]. How would that impact your business?"

Note that these questions are all focused on the other party - their needs, their perspective, and their definition of success. That's because the most effective negotiators know that it's not about them - it's about understanding and addressing the other side's interests.

Tips for Asking Questions Like a Ninja:

- Ask with genuine curiosity, not as a gotcha tactic

- Listen intently to the answers without interrupting or planning your response

- Follow up with additional questions to clarify or probe deeper

- Embrace the silence after asking a question - give them space to think and respond

- Avoid leading questions that suggest a "right" answer

By honing your questioning skills and prioritizing active listening, you'll be able to gather the information you need to craft solutions that truly resonate - and to build the kind of rapport that leads to long-term success.

Think of questions as keys that unlock hidden doors of opportunity. Each question you ask can reveal new insights, challenges, or possibilities you haven't considered before.

And the more keys you collect, the more doors you can open - doors to understanding, trust, creative problem-solving, and, ultimately, mutually beneficial agreements.

So channel your inner ninja, embrace your curiosity, and ask questions that unlock breakthrough insights and outcomes. Because sometimes, the answer you need isn't in the response - it's in the question itself.

***

How to Make Them Feel Like You're Their Long-Lost Best Friend

Picture this: you're in a negotiation, and your counterparts are from completely different worlds—different industries, backgrounds, maybe even countries. You're struggling to find any common ground, and the tension is thicker than your grandma's gravy.

What do you do? Do you accept defeat and resign yourself to an awkward, adversarial negotiation?

Absolutely not. You really connect with them, making it feel like you're the long-lost best friend they never knew they had.

The Psychology of Mirroring

The secret to instant rapport is a technique called mirroring. The idea is simple: people like people who are like them. We're drawn to others who share our mannerisms, our speech patterns, and even our body language.

By subtly mirroring your counterpart's behavior, you send a subconscious signal that says, "Hey, I'm just like you!" This creates a sense of familiarity and trust, even if you've just met.

How to Mirror Effectively:

- Match their tone and pace of speech (but don't mimic them word for word - that's just creepy)

- Adopt similar body language and posture (if they lean in, you lean in)

- Use the same keywords and phrases they use (if they say "deal," you say "deal")

The key is to be subtle. You don't want to come off as a parrot or a stalker. Just aim for a natural, comfortable synchronicity, like old friends who finish each other's sentences.

Tips for Building Rapport Naturally:

Mirroring is a great foundation, but true rapport goes deeper. Here are some tips for taking your connection to the next level:

- Express genuine interest in their perspective. Ask questions, listen intently, and show that you value their insights.

- Find small points of agreement early on. Even if it's just a shared love of coffee or a mutual disdain for Monday meetings, highlighting commonalities helps build a bond.

- Use humor and storytelling to create a sense of warmth and authenticity. Share a funny anecdote or a relatable struggle - it'll make you seem more human and approachable.

Think of rapport-building as reconnecting with a long-lost friend. Although you might not have seen each other in years, you quickly fall into old patterns, laugh at inside jokes, and remember why you clicked in the first place.

Just like with an old friend, rapport is founded on a genuine interest in and care for the other person. It's not about manipulation or fakery—it's about finding authentic ways to relate, empathize, and connect.

So the next time you find yourself in a negotiation with a seeming stranger, channel your inner bestie. Mirror their mannerisms, find common ground, and show them that despite your differences, you're more alike than they realize.

Who knows? By the end of the negotiation, you might walk away with a great deal - and a new BFF to boot.

Finding Common Ground, Even If It's Just a Shared Love of Coffee

Alright, so you've mastered the art of mirroring and are well on your way to becoming your counterpart's new best friend. But what happens when, despite your best efforts, you still need help finding any common ground? When it feels like you're negotiating with an alien from another planet?

First, take a deep breath. It's okay. Even the most skilled negotiators sometimes encounter a counterpart who seems to have nothing in common with them. The key is not to panic, but to get creative.

Why Common Ground Matters

Before we dive into how to find common ground, let's talk about why it matters. In a word: trust. Establishing even a small point of connection with your counterpart, it builds a foundation of trust and goodwill that can carry you through the toughest parts of the negotiation.

Think about it: if you discovered that your counterpart shared your obsession with Game of Thrones, or that you both ran the same 10k last year, wouldn't that make you feel more at ease? A little more like you're dealing with a real human being, not just a name on a contract.

That's the power of common ground. It humanizes the negotiation and opens the door to more authentic, collaborative conversations.

How to Find Common Ground in Even the Toughest Situations

Okay, so you won't bond over your shared love of skydiving or your mutual hatred of pineapple on pizza. That doesn't mean all hope is lost.

Here are some tips for uncovering common ground, even in the most challenging negotiations:

1. Look for universal human experiences. Even if you come from different cultures or industries, there are certain experiences that unite us all—things like the love of family, the desire for respect, or the fear of failure. By tapping into these universal themes, you can find a point of connection that transcends surface differences.

2. Ask about their story. Everyone has a unique journey that brought them to the negotiation table. You may uncover surprising points of similarity by showing genuine interest in your counterpart's background, motivations, and aspirations. Maybe you both started your careers in a totally different field, or you both had a teacher who changed your life. These shared stories create a bond that can carry you through the negotiation.

3. Find a common enemy. Okay, enemy might be a strong word. But sometimes, the quickest way to build rapport is to unite against a shared challenge or frustration. You may be both trying to navigate a complex regulatory environment or fed up with the slow pace of change in your industry. By commiserating over a common pain point, you create an "us against the world" dynamic that can be surprisingly powerful.

4. When all else fails, there's always coffee. Or tea. Or whatever beverage you both enjoy. Never underestimate the power of a shared love of caffeine to break the ice and establish a basic human connection.

The Bottom Line

At the end of the day, finding common ground is about remembering that the person across the table is just that - a person. Like you, they have hopes, fears, quirks, and passions. And even if you come from wildly different worlds, there's always some connection to be found - if you're willing to look for it.

So the next time you struggle to find common ground, don't give up. Keep searching for that shared story, that common frustration, that universal human experience. And in the worst-case scenario, invite them out for a cup of coffee. You might be surprised at how quickly a shared love of lattes can turn adversaries into allies.

And who knows? By the end of the negotiation, you might have a new addition to your professional network - and your coffee klatch.

Conclusion

Active listening is the unsung hero of negotiation. It's not flashy, it's not always easy, and it doesn't get the same attention as slick closing techniques or power poses.

But make no mistake: active listening is the foundation of all successful negotiations. It's how you uncover hidden needs, build genuine rapport, and find creative solutions that leave everyone feeling heard and valued.

So as you go forth and conquer your next negotiation, remember the power of being present. Put down your phone, set aside your agenda, and tune into what your counterpart is saying - and what they're not saying.

Ask questions that unlock new insights. Mirror their behavior to build a subconscious bond. And never stop searching for that common ground, even if it's as simple as a shared love of a good cuppa joe.

Because when you master the art of active listening, you become more than just a skilled negotiator. You become a trusted partner, a creative problem-solver, and maybe even a lifelong friend.

And that, my dear reader, is a superpower worth cultivating. So go forth and listen like your life depends on it. Your negotiation success (and your coffee buddy) will thank you.

Chapter Four

Mastering the Language of Persuasion

Words are your most powerful weapon in negotiation. The right words can build bridges, close deals, and leave everyone feeling like they've won. In this chapter, you'll learn how to turn phrases into connection builders, objections into opportunities, and even awkward silences into moments of persuasion mastery.

Using "You" Statements to Create Connection Because It's Not About You, It's About Them

Let's be honest - we've all been that person at a party who can't stop talking about themselves. It's exhausting, right? Well, the same principle applies to negotiations. Too often, we get so caught up in our own agenda that we forget the cardinal rule of persuasion: it's not about you; it's about them.

When you walk into a negotiation armed with a meticulously prepared pitch about your company's mission statement and your own impressive resume, you're essentially that party guest who won't stop yammering on about their latest vacation photos. And trust me, no one wants to be that person.

So, what's the secret to avoiding this negotiation faux pas? Make every conversation, every proposal, and every question about them. Be the detective who uncovers what truly matters to your counterpart.

The Psychology of Focusing on "You"

Focusing on "you" rather than "I" makes the other party feel understood and valued. It shows that you're not just there to push your own agenda but to understand and address their needs truly. When people feel heard and understood, they're more likely to trust you, engage in collaborative problem-solving, and ultimately say "yes" to your proposals.

Examples of Effective "You" Statements

- "You'll see immediate results from this approach."

- "This solution will make your life easier."

- "You mentioned that increasing sales is a top priority. Here's how our product can help you achieve that goal."

Notice how each of these statements focuses squarely on the other person and their needs. They're not about how great you or your product are but about how you can improve your counterpart's life.

Tips for Shifting Focus to the Other Person

1. Replace self-centered phrases with audience-centered ones.

   ○ Instead of: "I think this is a great opportunity."

   ○ Try: "You'll see a significant return on investment with this approach."

2. Use inclusive language that demonstrates shared goals.

   ○ Instead of: "If you buy from me, I'll exceed my quota."

   ○ Try: "By partnering together, we can help you crush your targets and make us both look like rock stars."

3. Channel your inner superhero storyteller.

- Think of yourself as the narrator of their success story. Your role is to guide them, support them, and ultimately help them emerge victorious. By positioning yourself as their ally and advocate rather than just another salesperson, you'll build trust, rapport, and the kind of connection that leads to long-term success.

So, the next time you slip into "I" mode, pause, take a breath, and flip the script. Ask yourself, "How can I make this about them?" Because when you master the art of the "you," you'll be amazed at how quickly "no" turns into "yes."

***

How to Name-Drop Like a Pro

Alright, let's talk about that person we all know - the one who can't make it through a single conversation without casually mentioning their "dear friend" Elon Musk or their recent "power lunch" with Sheryl Sandberg. It's tempting to roll your eyes and tune out, but here's the thing: when done right, social proof can be a powerful tool in your negotiation toolkit.

Why People Trust Social Proof and Authority

We're wired to trust the opinions and experiences of others, especially those we perceive as successful or authoritative. When you mention that you've worked with big-name clients or have been endorsed by industry leaders, you're tapping into that deep-rooted psychological principle. Suddenly, your counterpart isn't just taking your word for it; they're thinking, "Well, if it worked for Company X or Expert Y, it must be legit."

Examples of Leveraging Social Proof

- Mentioning similar clients or industries: "We've helped companies like ABC Corp and XYZ Inc achieve some pretty impressive results."

- Referencing data or testimonials: "In a recent survey, 95% of our clients reported a significant increase in productivity after implementing our solution."

- Highlighting endorsements or awards: "We're proud to have been named Best in Class by the Industry Experts Association for the past three years running."

The key is to make your social proof relevant, specific, and authentic. Don't just drop names for the sake of impressing; share examples that speak directly to your counterpart's unique needs and challenges.

How to Position Yourself as an Authority Without Being Arrogant

There's a fine line between leveraging your expertise and coming across as a braggadocious know-it-all. The secret is to let your credentials and experience speak for themselves, rather than constantly tooting your own horn.

1. Use facts and data to subtly underscore your authority.

   ○ Instead of: "I'm the leading expert in this field."

   ○ Try: "Studies from Harvard Business Review and McKinsey have shown that this approach leads to a 25% increase in ROI."

2. Highlight your experience through storytelling.

   ○ Instead of: "I've been doing this for 20 years and have seen it all."

   ○ Try: "Just last month, I worked with a client facing a similar challenge. Here's how we tackled it and what we learned."

3. Embrace a touch of self-deprecating humor.

  ○ "I don't like to brag, but I once won a 'World's Okayest Negotiator' coffee mug. So, you know, I'm kind of a big deal."

The point is, that you don't need to shove your resume in your counterpart's face to establish your credibility. By naturally weaving your expertise into the conversation, you'll build trust and authority without sacrificing likability.

And remember, it's not bragging if it's true - and it's not name-dropping if it works. So go forth and sprinkle those social proof points like the seasoned pro you are. Just don't be surprised if people start name-dropping you in their own negotiations.

***

Framing Offers in Terms of Benefits Because Nobody Cares About Features, They Want Results

Quick pop quiz: When's the last time you got super jazzed about a product's technical specs? Unless you're a total tech geek (no judgment), probably never. And guess what? Your clients feel the same way.

Here's the deal: People don't buy features; they buy better versions of themselves. They don't care about your product's bells and whistles; they care about how it will transform their business, simplify their lives, and help them achieve their wildest dreams (okay, maybe not that last one, but you get the point).

Features vs. Benefits: What's the Diff?

Imagine you're trying to sell a snazzy new project management software. You could ramble on about its automated Gantt charts, drag-and-drop interface, and built-in analytics engine. But let's be real - your client's eyes are glazing over faster than a Krispy Kreme donut.

Now, imagine instead that you said, "With our software, you'll be able to streamline your workflows, collaborate seamlessly with your team, and gain real-time visibility into your projects. No more missed deadlines, no more communication breakdowns, and no more late nights at the office. You'll be the productivity superhero your company needs."

Boom. Mic drop.

The difference? You've translated the features into tangible, compelling benefits. You've painted a picture of how your product will improve their work life and make it more fun.

Techniques for Translating Features into Benefits

1. Ask yourself, "So what?"

   - Take each feature and ask, "So what? Why should my client care about this? What's in it for them?"

   - Keep drilling down until you get to the core benefit.

   - Example: "Our software integrates with over 200 third-party apps."   "So what?"   "You can seamlessly connect all your favorite tools."   "So what?"   "Your team can work faster and more efficiently, without the headache of switching between platforms."

2. Link benefits to specific pain points.

   - Before the negotiation, do your homework to uncover your counterpart's biggest challenges, frustrations, and goals.

- Then, frame your benefits as the antidote to those pain points.

- Example: "You mentioned that you're struggling with version control and missed deadlines. With our real-time collaboration features and automated reminders, you'll never have to worry about those issues again."

3. Paint a vivid picture.

- Use concrete examples and storytelling to help your counterpart visualize the benefits in action.

- Transport them to a world where your product has already solved their problems and improved their lives.

- Example: "Imagine this: It's Friday afternoon, and your team is wrapping up work on a major client project. In the past, this would have meant a frantic scramble to integrate everyone's changes and get the final deliverable out the door. But with our software, everything is seamlessly synced in the cloud. You can see who's done what at a glance, review and approve with just a click, and send off the final product with time to spare. No stress, no drama, just sweet, sweet success."

The Result? Closed Deals and Happy Clients

When focusing on benefits rather than features, you speak your counterpart's language. You show them that you understand their world, their challenges, and their aspirations. You position yourself not just as another vendor but as a strategic partner invested in their success.

And here's the best part: When you get good at this whole "benefits" thing, your clients will start selling themselves. They'll hear your pitch and think, "Yes, that's exactly what I need!" They'll be ready to sign on the dotted line before you even finish your sentence.

So, the next time you're tempted to geek out over your product's specs, remember: It ain't about the features, my friend. It's about the benefits - the juicy, life-changing, deal-closing benefits.

And if all else fails? Just throw in a free pizza party with every purchase. Trust me, it works every time.

Handling Objections with Grace and a Dash of Wit

Ah, objections. They're like the mosquitoes of the negotiation world - annoying, persistent, and always showing up when you least expect them. But here's the thing: Objections aren't roadblocks; they're opportunities. They're little windows into your counterpart's mind, inviting you to peer inside, understand their concerns, and craft a solution to blow their socks off.

Why Objections Are Opportunities in Disguise

When your client raises an objection, they're not saying "no" - they're saying "I'm not convinced yet." They're telling you that there's a gap between what you're offering and what they need. Your job, as the master negotiator, is to bridge that gap with empathy, creativity, and a touch of moxie.

The Three-Step Objection Handling Tango

1. Listen without interrupting.

   - Resist the urge to jump in with a pre-packaged rebuttal.

   - Let your counterpart fully express their concern, without judgment or defensiveness.

   - Show that you're fully present and engaged through active listening cues like nodding, eye contact, and the occasional "mmhmm."

2. Acknowledge their concern with empathy.

- Repeat back what you heard to show that you understand their perspective.

- Validate their concern as legitimate and reasonable.

- Use phrases like "I hear you," "That's a valid point," or "I can see how that could be a concern."

3. Respond with a solution or reassurance.

- Offer a specific, tailored response that addresses their concern head-on.

- Provide evidence, examples, or guarantees to back up your solution.

- Frame your response as a collaborative effort to find a mutually beneficial outcome.

***

Handling Objections with Grace and a Dash of Wit

Let's be real - objection handling can get a little tense sometimes. Emotions run high, egos get bruised, and suddenly everyone's talking in that weird, formal "negotiation voice." But here's a little secret: A well-placed dash of humor can work wonders to defuse the tension and create a more collaborative vibe.

1. Use wit to acknowledge the elephant in the room.

- Example: "I know our price might seem as intimidating as a root canal without novocaine. But hear me out - we're easy to work with and much better for your business in the long run.."

2. Poke fun at common objections in a relatable way.

- Example: "I get it - budgets are tighter than skinny jeans after Thanksgiving dinner. But what if I told you there's a way to get the results you want without busting your seams?"

3. Turn the objection into a shared mission.

- Example: "You're right, our timeline is about as tight as a clown car at the circus. But hey, if we can pull this off, we'll be legends! Whaddya say - ready to join forces and make some magic happen?"

Of course, humor is a delicate dance. Read the room, know your audience, and when in doubt, stay on the professional side. But don't be afraid to let your personality shine through - it's what makes you human, relatable, and trustworthy.

Putting It All Together

Let's take a step back and look at the big picture. Objection handling is not about "winning" or getting your way. It's about understanding your counterpart's needs, addressing their concerns, and finding a solution that works for everyone.

So, the next time you encounter an objection, don't panic. Take a deep breath, summon your inner negotiation ninja, and remember: This is your moment to shine. Listen with empathy, respond creatively, and don't be afraid to sprinkle in a little wit along the way.

And if all else fails? Just remember the wise words of the great philosopher Michael Scott: "Sometimes I'll start a [negotiation], and I don't even know where it's going. I just hope I find it along the way."

Happy objection handling, my friends. May your rebuttals be sharp, your solutions brilliant, and your one-liners legendary.

Whew, that was a wild ride through the wonderful world of persuasive language, wasn't it? We've covered everything from the power of "you" statements to the art of the well-timed name-drop, the magic of benefit-driven framing, to the joys of witty objection handling.

But here's the thing - mastering the language of persuasion isn't just about memorizing a bunch of clever phrases or slick tactics. It's about genuinely connecting with your counterpart, understanding their needs and concerns, and finding creative ways to craft mutually beneficial solutions.

So, as you go forth and negotiate, keep these key principles in mind:

1. Make it about them, not you.

2. Let your social proof do the talking.

3. Sell the sizzle, not the steak.

4. Handle objections with empathy and grace (and maybe a sprinkle of humor).

And above all, remember that persuasion isn't about manipulation or trickery - it's about building trust, rapport, and relationships that stand the test of time. Because at the end of the day, the most persuasive thing you can be is authentically, unapologetically you.

So go forth and persuade, my friends. Use your words wisely, listen with intent, and never underestimate the power of a well-timed pun. The negotiation world is your oyster - now go forth and shuck it.

(And if you ever need a little moral support, just remember - I'm rootin' for ya, kid. Follow these rules, you can negotiate anything.)

Chapter Five

The Power of Timing and Silence

They say timing is everything, and negotiation is no exception. What if you could make someone sweat with a well-timed pause or steer a deal in your favor just by knowing when to speak up—or stay quiet? In this chapter, you'll learn how to use timing and silence to your advantage, leaving others wondering how you became such a negotiation ninja.

Knowing When to Speak and When to Listen Because Sometimes Silence Is Truly Golden

Picture this: you're in the heat of a negotiation, and you can feel the tension rising. Your counterpart is getting agitated, their words coming faster and more forcefully. Every fiber of your being is screaming at you to jump in, defend your position, and prove them wrong. But wait - what if the key to winning this battle is not in what you say but what you don't?

Enter the power of active listening. It may seem counterintuitive, but sometimes, the best way to gain the upper hand in a negotiation is to simply shut up and listen. By giving your counterparts the space to express themselves fully, you're gathering valuable information about their needs and motivations and building trust and rapport.

But how do you know when to speak up and when to zip it? Here are a few ninja tips:

Wait for the right cues.

- Is your counterpart asking for your input or opinion?

- Have they paused expectantly, signaling it's your turn to chime in?

- Has the conversation reached a natural lull?

These are all good indicators that it's time for you to speak your piece.

Resist the urge to fill the silence.

- We've all been there - that awkward moment when the conversation grinds to a halt, and the silence feels deafening.

- Your instinct might be to jump in with whatever comes to mind, just to break the tension.

- But resist that urge! Embrace the silence, and let your counterpart be the one to fill it. You might be surprised at what they reveal when given the space.

Use body language to show you're listening.

- Active listening isn't just about staying quiet - it's about fully engaging with what your counterpart is saying.

- You can show that you're paying attention by maintaining eye contact, nodding at appropriate moments, and maintaining an open, relaxed posture.

- Avoid crossing your arms, checking your phone, or letting your gaze wander - these are all surefire signs that you're mentally checked out.

Reflect back on what you've heard.

- One of the most powerful ways to show you're listening is to paraphrase your counterpart's key points and then repeat them.

- This demonstrates that you're paying attention and allows you to clarify any misunderstandings and ensure you're on the same page.

- Try starting with phrases like, "So what I'm hearing is..." or "It sounds like your main concern is..."

Mastering the art of active listening will make your negotiations go much more smoothly. Think of it as channeling your inner Zen master. You create an atmosphere of trust and collaboration by staying calm, present, and focused on understanding rather than just being understood. And who knows? You might find that your counterpart talks themselves right into a deal that works for everyone.

***

How to Make Them Sweat Without Saying a Word

Alright, you've mastered the art of active listening. You know when to speak up, and more importantly, when to zip it. But what if I told you that the real power move in a negotiation isn't just staying quiet - it's harnessing the power of the pause?

That's right, my ninja friend. The well-timed pause is a secret weapon that can make even the most seasoned negotiator break a sweat. Why? Because silence is uncomfortable. It creates tension, ratchets up the pressure, and forces the other party to confront their own thoughts and doubts. And if you can learn to wield that discomfort to your advantage, you'll be unstoppable.

So how do you effectively use pauses in a negotiation? Here are a few techniques:

1. Drop a bombshell, then wait.

    ◦ Have a game-changing piece of information or a bold proposal to share? Don't just blurt it out and keep rambling.

    ◦ Deliver your bombshell, then sit back and let the silence do the work.

    ◦ Watch as your counterpart processes the information, and resist the urge to fill the space with unnecessary explanations or justifications.

2. Ask a probing question, then listen.

    ◦ The only thing more powerful than a well-timed pause? A well-timed question followed by a pause.

    ◦ Ask your counterpart something that makes them think - about their priorities, concerns, or bottom line.

    ◦ Then wait. Give them space to formulate a thoughtful response, and watch as the information you need to negotiate effectively comes spilling out.

3. Make an offer, then be still.

    ◦ When you're ready to put a deal on the table, do it with confidence - and then stop talking.

    ◦ Don't undercut your own offer by immediately backtracking or offering concessions.

    ◦ Let your proposal hang in the air, and give your counterpart time to consider it. More often than not, they'll be the ones to blink first.

But a word of warning: like any powerful tool, the pause must be used wisely. Overdo it, and you risk coming across as manipulative or awkward. The key is to deploy your pauses strategically, in moments when they'll have the most impact.

Think of pauses like the dramatic beats in a movie - they work best when they're used sparingly, to punctuate key moments and keep the audience engaged. Used correctly, a pause can be the difference between a boring, predictable negotiation and a heart-pounding, edge-of-your-seat thriller.

So the next time you're in the negotiation hot seat, remember: sometimes, the most powerful thing you can say is nothing at all. Embrace the discomfort, let the silence work its magic, and watch as your counterpart sweat - while you keep your cool.

***

Creating a Sense of Urgency Without Being the Annoying Car Salesman

We've all been there - cornered by a pushy salesperson who just won't take no for an answer. They're all about creating a sense of urgency, piling on the pressure, and making us feel like we'll miss out on the deal of a lifetime if we don't sign on the dotted line right this second.

It's annoying, right? But here's the thing: when used correctly, a sense of urgency can be a powerful tool in negotiation. The key is to create that urgency authentically, without resorting to high-pressure tactics or manipulation.

So how do you walk that fine line? It all comes down to tapping into your counterpart's motivations and priorities. Here are a few techniques:

1. Highlight the benefits of acting sooner rather than later.

- Instead of arbitrary deadlines or limited-time offers, focus on the tangible advantages your counterpart will gain by moving forward now.

- For example: "If we can come to an agreement this week, you'll be able to start realizing the cost savings by the start of next quarter."

- By framing urgency in terms of their goals and priorities, you create a sense of positive momentum rather than external pressure.

2. Emphasize natural, time-sensitive opportunities.

- Is there an upcoming event, season, or project milestone that aligns perfectly with your proposal? Use it to your advantage!

- For example: "With the holiday shopping season right around the corner, now is the perfect time to implement our inventory management system. You'll be able to handle the increased demand with ease and maximize your profits."

- By tying your proposal to external timelines that are already on your counterpart's radar, you create a sense of urgency that feels organic rather than forced.

3. Use milestones to create a sense of scarcity.

- People are motivated by the fear of missing out or FOMO. You can use this to your advantage by highlighting key milestones or benchmarks that your counterpart won't want to miss.

- For example: "Our beta testing program is filling up fast, and we only have a few spots left. If we can finalize our partnership by the end of the month, I can guarantee you'll be part of the first cohort to get access to our new features."

- By creating a sense of scarcity or exclusivity around key

milestones, you tap into your counterpart's natural desire to be part of something special.

But here's the most important thing to remember: urgency should never be about pressuring your counterpart to make a decision they're not comfortable with. It's about highlighting the genuine benefits of acting sooner rather than later and aligning your proposal with their existing priorities and timelines.

Think of it like a gentle nudge in the right direction, not a shove off a cliff. If you find yourself resorting to high-pressure tactics or ultimatums, take a step back and reevaluate. Chances are, there's a more authentic way to create urgency that will leave everyone feeling good about the deal.

So the next time you're tempted to channel your inner used car salesman, remember: true urgency comes from within, not from external pressure. Focus on your counterpart's goals and priorities, highlight the natural advantages of acting sooner, and let the FOMO do the rest. You might be surprised at how quickly a "maybe" turns into a "let's do this."

***

Recognizing When to Walk Away Because Sometimes the Best Deal Is No Deal at All

Let's face it: as much as we all love a good negotiation, there comes a point in every deal where you must ask yourself - is this worth it? Is the juice worth the squeeze, or am I just spinning my wheels trying to make something work that's ultimately not in my best interest?

It's a tough call, but sometimes the most powerful move you can make in a negotiation is to walk away. Yes, you heard me right. Sometimes, no deal is better than a bad deal.

But how do you know when it's time to cut your losses and move on? Here are a few signs to watch out for:

1. The other party is unwilling to budge.

   - You've tried every technique in your negotiation toolkit - active listening, strategic pauses, creating urgency - but your counterpart just won't meet you halfway.

   - They're stuck in their position, unwilling to make any concessions or explore creative solutions.

   - At a certain point, you must ask yourself: is this a long-term partner I want to work with? If they're this inflexible now, what happens when inevitable challenges arise down the road?

2. The deal doesn't align with your values or priorities.

   - You could start out the negotiation with a clear idea of what success looked like - a certain price point, a specific set of terms, or a collaboration that felt mutually beneficial.

   - But as the conversation progressed, you realized that the deal on the table just doesn't align with your core values or long-term goals.

   - It's easy to get caught up in the heat of the moment and the desire to "win," but if a deal doesn't feel right in your gut, it's okay to walk away.

3. The costs outweigh the benefits.

   - Every deal has a certain set of trade-offs - time, resources, opportunity costs.

   - And while it's normal to make sacrifices for a greater goal, there comes a point where the scales tip too far in the wrong direction.

- If you find yourself pouring more and more into a deal while getting less and less in return, it might be time to cut your losses and redirect your energy elsewhere.

But, walking away from a deal doesn't have to be a scorched-earth situation. In fact, sometimes the most strategic way to walk away is to leave the door open for future collaboration. Here are a few tips:

1. Communicate your decision clearly and respectfully.

    - Don't just ghost your counterpart or leave them hanging.

    - Let them know that while you appreciate the time and effort they've put into the negotiation, you've ultimately decided the deal isn't the right fit for you at this time.

    - Be clear about your reasoning, but avoid placing blame or burning bridges.

2. Offer alternative solutions or referrals if appropriate.

    - Just because this particular deal didn't work out doesn't mean you can't support your counterpart in other ways.

    - If you have alternative solutions or referrals that better suit their needs, offer to make an introduction or share resources.

    - This shows you're still invested in their success, even if you won't work together directly.

3. Keep the lines of communication open.

    - You never know when circumstances might change or new opportunities might arise.

    - By ending the negotiation on a positive note and keeping the lines of communication open, you create space for future collaboration if and when the timing is right.

- A simple "please don't hesitate to reach out if anything changes" can go a long way in preserving goodwill and keeping doors open.

Walking away from a deal is never easy, but it's a crucial skill for any negotiation ninja to master. It's about knowing your worth, staying true to your values, and being willing to prioritize your long-term success over short-term gains.

So the next time you find yourself in a negotiation that isn't going anywhere, remember: walking away isn't losing. It's recognizing that your time, energy, and resources are valuable - and that sometimes, the best deal is the one you don't make.

Trust your gut, communicate with respect, and keep moving forward. Because in the grand scheme of things, every "no" is just a step closer to the right "yes" - even if you can't see it yet.

And there you have it, my ninja friends - the art of timing and silence in all its strategic glory. We've covered everything from the power of active listening to the art of the well-timed pause, the secrets of authentic urgency to the wisdom of knowing when to walk away.

But here's the thing: mastering timing and silence isn't just about deploying a set of tactics or tricks. It's about developing a deep understanding of your own goals and values, as well as those of your counterpart. It's about staying present and attuned to the subtle cues and shifts in the negotiation dance and adapting your approach accordingly.

And most importantly? It's about trusting your instincts and embracing the discomfort that comes with strategic silence or tough decisions. Because let's face it - negotiation is rarely a cakewalk. It's a high-stakes, high-pressure game that requires skills, courage, and emotional intelligence.

But with the tools and techniques we've explored in this chapter, you'll be well-equipped to navigate even the most challenging negotiation landscapes. You'll know when to speak up and when to listen, when to create urgency and when to back off, when to push forward, and when to walk away.

And through it all, you'll remember that the ultimate goal of negotiation isn't just to "win" in the short term - it's to build strong, mutually beneficial relationships that stand the test of time. Because when you approach negotiation with a spirit of collaboration, creativity, and genuine care for your counterpart's needs and goals, amazing things can happen.

So go forth and negotiate, my ninjas. Embrace the power of timing and silence, and use it to create deals that work for everyone involved. And remember - even the most skilled negotiators are always learning and growing. Every conversation is an opportunity to refine your skills, deepen your understanding, and become the kind of negotiator others aspire to be.

The world of negotiation is full of twists and turns, challenges and opportunities. But with your newfound mastery of timing and silence, you'll be ready to face whatever comes your way - one strategic pause at a time.

Chapter Six

Negotiating in the Digital Age

Picture this: You're about to close the biggest deal of your career. You've practiced your pitch, polished your proposal, and dressed for success – at least above the waist. Welcome to negotiating in 2024, where your home office is your war room and your internet connection is your lifeline to success.

How to Be a Ninja Over Zoom

Let me share something that still makes me cringe. Last year, I was leading a crucial negotiation with a potential investor. My presentation was flawless, my numbers were solid, and my confidence was high. Then it happened – my video froze just as I was making my power move. When I reconnected, my virtual background had failed, revealing my daughter's unicorn-themed wall art behind me. Not exactly the executive presence I was going for.

But here's the thing: virtual negotiations are here to stay, and mastering them is no longer optional. It's about turning potential pitfalls into strategic advantages. With some preparation and practice, you can create a virtual command center that showcases your professionalism and sets the stage for success.

Creating Your Virtual Command Center:

- Lighting: Position yourself facing natural light or invest in a ring light. Remember, you want to look like a negotiation ninja, not someone being interrogated under a bare bulb.

- Camera setup: Keep it at eye level – your colleagues don't need a view up your nostrils or a fascinating study of your ceiling fan. Consider your camera your conversation partner.

- Background: Choose something professional but not sterile. A bookshelf or plain wall works perfectly. (Save your Star Wars poster collection for after you close the deal.)

- Audio quality: Invest in a good microphone. "Can you hear me now?" is not a power phrase in negotiations.

But it's not just about the technical setup. Your virtual presence is equally important. Just like in-person negotiations, your body language speaks volumes. Here's how to make sure it's sending the right message:

Virtual Body Language That Wins:

1. Master the art of digital eye contact by looking directly at your camera when speaking

2. Keep your gestures controlled and purposeful – visible but not distracting

3. Maintain good posture without looking like you swallowed a broomstick

4. Use deliberate nodding and facial expressions to show engagement (without turning into a bobblehead)

Pro Tip: Record yourself in a practice session. Yes, it's awkward. Yes, you'll cringe. And yes, it's absolutely worth it to see how you come across on screen. Consider it your personal dress rehearsal before the big show.

Navigating the Virtual Dojo

Virtual negotiations strip us of the full range of nonverbal cues we rely on in face-to-face interactions. This limitation requires us to be more precise in our communication and more expressive in ways that can be captured on camera. It's about making your visible actions speak louder than words.

Managing Distractions and Technical Glitches

In the virtual world, distractions are just a click away, and technical issues can arise like sudden attacks. Have backup plans for internet issues, such as a mobile hotspot, and keep distractions at bay by informing others of your important meeting.

Managing Screen Fatigue

To combat the drain of long sessions, structure your negotiations with short, focused bursts of discussion followed by breaks. This keeps everyone's energy up and attention sharp. Consider also using engaging visuals like slides or charts to keep the conversation lively and grounded in your objectives.

Think of virtual negotiations as ninjitsu on a screen—you're invisible, but still in control. Just as a ninja uses the shadows to their advantage, they use the virtual setting to control the flow of information and the pace of the negotiation. Your screen is your dojo, your preparation is your katana, and your adaptability is your shuriken.

By mastering these elements, you transform from a mere participant into a formidable digital negotiator, capable of turning any virtual challenge to your advantage. Embrace the path of the screen ninja, and lead your negotiations with stealth and precision.

Leveraging Technology to Your Advantage Because Even Ninjas Need Tech Support Sometimes

Remember the days when negotiation prep meant walking into a room with a stack of papers and a prayer? Today's digital toolkit gives us capabilities that would make previous generations of negotiators weep with joy. But like any powerful tool, it's all about how you use it.

Think of technology as your trusty sidekick - there to support you, but not steal the show. Used strategically, it can help you research, prepare, and present like a pro. Here's what you need in your digital arsenal:

Essential Digital Arsenal

Document Management:

- Cloud storage for instant access to crucial files

- Digital signature tools for seamless closing

- Real-time collaboration platforms for live edits

These tools ensure you're never caught off guard, fumbling for a file, or scrambling to incorporate last-minute changes. With everything at your fingertips, you can focus on what matters - the negotiation itself.

Research Tools:

- LinkedIn Sales Navigator for background intelligence

- Industry databases for market insights

- CRM systems for relationship tracking

Knowledge is power, and these tools give you the intel you need to confidently walk into any negotiation. From understanding your counterpart's background to staying on top of market trends, you'll be the most prepared person in the (virtual) room.

<u>Presentation Tools:</u>

- Interactive slide decks that engage rather than bore

- Virtual whiteboards for collaborative problem-solving

- Screen-sharing capabilities for dynamic demonstrations

Gone are the days of death by PowerPoint. Today's presentation tools let you bring your ideas to life, making your pitch more engaging and persuasive. Used well, they can be the difference between a yawn and a "yes."

How Technology Can Streamline Preparation

Leverage apps and tools not just for basic tasks but as strategic assets in your negotiation prep. Apps like **Evernote** or CRM software can be used for meticulous research and note-taking, organizing your thoughts and strategies into one accessible location. Set up automated reminders for follow-ups and deadlines, ensuring nothing slips through the cracks.

Strategies for Using Technology During Negotiations

In the heat of negotiation, technology should be your silent partner. Use tools to share documents seamlessly, reducing friction and maintaining the flow of discussion. Employ digital whiteboards or shared documents for real-time collaboration, allowing all parties to contribute and amend proposals on the fly, creating a dynamic and interactive negotiation environment.

Avoiding Over-Reliance on Tech

While tech can greatly enhance your negotiation capabilities, it's vital not to become overly reliant on it. Always have a backup plan for tech failures—whether it's alternative communication channels or hard copies of crucial documents. Strive to maintain a human connection by balancing technological aids with genuine interaction—remember, your gadgets are there to enhance your presentation, not overshadow it.

Even ninjas occasionally rely on gadgets—just make sure your tech doesn't steal the show. It's about using technology as a bridge, not a barrier, connecting ideas and people rather than creating distances. Your role is to orchestrate these tools to amplify your negotiation prowess, ensuring they enhance your skills rather than replace the human element that is crucial to successful negotiations.

The key is to let technology enhance, not dominate, your negotiation. Think of it as your utility belt – helpful tools at the ready, but not the main show. Remember, at the end of the day, your skills and presence close the deal.

***

Maintaining Rapport and Trust Online Without Resorting to Awkward Virtual High-Fives

Building trust through a screen can feel as natural as dancing at a wedding with your in-laws. But here's the truth: virtual rapport isn't just possible; it can be as powerful as in-person connections. You just need to master the art of digital charisma.

Think about it this way: every interaction, no matter how small, is an opportunity to strengthen your relationship. You're setting the tone from the moment that calendar invite goes out. Here's how to make it count:

Creating Your Digital First Impression

<u>Pre-Meeting Magic:</u>

- Send a warm, personalized agenda that shows you value their time

- Share relevant materials early (because nobody enjoys rushing through documents live)

- Connect on LinkedIn thoughtfully – think "professional handshake," not "desperate stalker"

These small touches demonstrate that you're prepared, considerate, and, most importantly, human. They lay the groundwork for a productive and positive interaction, setting a tone that values respect and professionalism.

<u>During the Meeting:</u>

- Start with genuine, light conversation – but please, no weather talk unless you're negotiating with a meteorologist

- Use names naturally and often

- Reference shared insights or experiences

- Stay present – multi-tasking is the virtual equivalent of checking your phone at dinner

This is where you build on that initial foundation. By showing genuine interest, finding common ground, and giving your full attention, you demonstrate that you value the relationship, not just the deal.

<u>Building Digital Trust:</u>

- Be impeccable with your commitments, no matter how small

- Address technical issues honestly – we're all human, even through screens

- Follow up promptly and personally

- Create consistent touchpoints between meetings

Trust is constructed in these small, consistent moments, often when least observed but most impactful. By showing dependability, honesty, and regular engagement, you're not just another contact—they see you as a dependable ally.

Challenges of Building Rapport Virtually:

- Lack of physical presence can make it harder to form a personal connection.

- Difficulty in reading body language requires a more expressive way to communicate sincerity and reaction, such as nodding, smiling, and using verbal affirmations to show you are engaged and empathetic.

Techniques to Build Trust and Rapport Online:

- Warm introductions and casual conversation at the start can set a friendly tone.

- Use humor or light anecdotes to break the ice, making the session less stiff and more approachable.

- To simulate direct interaction, maintain eye contact by looking at the camera, not the screen.

Staying focused on the conversation without distractions demonstrates your commitment to the interaction and respect for the other party involved.

Remember: Every interaction is a brick in your trust foundation. Make each one count. With patience, authenticity, and a bit of digital savvy, you can build connections that are just as strong online as they are in person.

***

Navigating Cross-Cultural Communication and Avoiding International Incidents

Here's a humbling moment: I once started negotiating with Japanese executives by giving an enthusiastic thumbs-up on camera. Little did I know that in some places, this gesture can be just as inappropriate as other well-known offensive hand signals. Talk about starting off on the wrong thumb.

In today's global marketplace, your morning might start with Beijing and end with Berlin. Cultural intelligence isn't just nice to have – it's essential for survival. But don't worry, you don't need to become a UN diplomat overnight. With a little research and a lot of respect, you can navigate the global stage with confidence.

Master the Art of Global Digital Diplomacy

<u>Time Zone Mastery:</u>

- Use tools like World Time Buddy to manage meetings across different time zones.

- Rotate meeting times fairly—everyone should share the burden of inconvenient meeting times.

- Be explicit about time zones in all communications to avoid confusion.

- Consider recording key sessions for asynchronous viewing to accommodate everyone.

Cultural Communication Strategies:

- Research cultural business norms before your first meeting. Understanding whether a culture values directness or prefers a more relational approach can shape how you prepare.

  - In some cultures, straightforward communication is appreciated and expected.

  - In others, there is greater emphasis on establishing relationships before discussing business.

- Learn basic greetings in your counterpart's language to show respect and effort.

- Pay attention to cultural holidays and business hours to avoid scheduling blunders.

Digital Etiquette Across Borders:

- Respect different approaches to decision-making, recognizing that some cultures may require more deliberation or consensus.

- Be patient with language barriers, using clear and simple language as much as possible.

- Consider cultural views on time and deadlines, as perceptions of punctuality can vary significantly.

- Adapt your humor carefully (what's funny in New York might flop in New Delhi)

Pro Tip: Keep a cultural cheat sheet for each region you work with. Mine includes notes like "No thumbs up in virtual meetings with Team Tokyo" and "Small talk is big business with Brazilian partners."

The Golden Rule of Global Negotiations

When in doubt, lean towards formality and respect. You can always relax your approach later, but recovering from a cultural misstep is hard. Remember, no one expects you to be perfect. Mistakes happen to the best of us. The key is approaching each interaction with curiosity, humility, and a genuine desire to learn.

Why Cultural Awareness Matters in the Digital Age

Negotiating with global teams or clients is more common than ever. Embracing cultural differences and demonstrating awareness can prevent misunderstandings and build stronger, more respectful business relationships.

Strategies for Bridging Cultural Gaps:

- Ask clarifying questions tactfully to ensure you fully understand the nuances of the conversation.

- Express interest and appreciation for cultural differences to build trust and rapport.

Think of yourself as a ninja diplomat—smoothly moving through different cultures without making any awkward mistakes. Your digital diplomacy can connect different worlds, making you a valuable negotiator who not only appreciates cultural differences but also uses them to enhance interactions and results.

The digital age has transformed how we negotiate, but the core principles remain the same: build rapport, stay adaptable, and always keep learning. Master these virtual skills, and you'll be ready to close deals from your living room or across the world. Just remember to double-check that unicorn background before your next big meeting.

Chapter Seven

Beyond the Boardroom: Negotiation in Everyday Life

Negotiation isn't just for CEOs and salespeople—it's a skill you use daily, whether you realize it or not. From convincing your partner to pick your dream vacation to haggling with your internet provider, this chapter proves that negotiation can make life smoother, happier, and maybe even a little more fun.

How to Get Your Significant Other to Agree to That Vacation

Picture this: You're daydreaming about white sandy beaches and crystal-clear waters, but your partner's idea of the perfect getaway involves more mountains than mai tais. It's the age-old vacation debate, and you're determined to come out on top (without ending up in the doghouse).

Here's the secret: negotiating with your significant other is all about finding that sweet spot where everyone feels like a winner.

Techniques for Negotiating at Home

1. Frame it as a win-win

Instead of focusing on what you want, highlight how your dream vacation benefits both of you. "If we go to the beach, you'll finally get to disconnect from work and relax, and I'll get to snorkel and explore the underwater world. It's a win-win!"

2. Listen to understand their perspective

Before diving into your pitch, take the time to genuinely listen to your partner's concerns and priorities. Maybe they're worried about the budget or have their heart set on a specific destination. By showing empathy and understanding, you lay the groundwork for a collaborative solution.

3. Time it right

Trying to negotiate when emotions are running high (like right after a stressful work day) is a recipe for disaster. Instead, wait for a moment when you feel calm, open, and receptive. It could be over a relaxing Sunday brunch or a casual evening stroll.

Real-Life Scenarios

Negotiating at home isn't just about big-ticket items like vacations. It's about navigating the daily dance of compromise and collaboration.

For example, let's say it's your turn to do the dishes, but you've had a long day and just want to curl up on the couch. Instead of whining or starting a fight, try a little playful negotiation: "Hey love, I know it's my night for dishes, but I'm exhausted. How about I give you a killer foot massage in exchange for taking my shift?"

Or maybe you're trying to decide where to order takeout. Instead of getting into a heated debate over pizza vs. sushi, approach it with curiosity and compromise: "I'm craving something spicy, but I know you're in the mood for comfort food. What if we do Thai tonight and save the pizza for our movie night this weekend?"

The Art of Ninja Diplomacy

At the end of the day, negotiating with your significant other is about more than getting your way—it's about strengthening your relationship. By approaching these conversations with empathy, creativity, and a touch of playfulness, you turn potential conflicts into opportunities for connection.

Think of it as ninja diplomacy, disguised as everyday conversation. With a little practice (and maybe a few well-timed foot rubs), you'll be amazed at how easy it becomes to find that sweet spot of mutual satisfaction.

So the next time you dream of that perfect beach getaway, remember: that you've got the tools to make it happen. And who knows? You may discover a whole new side of your partner in the process.

✷✷✷

Negotiating with Service Providers and Vendors Because Even Ninjas Need to Haggle Sometimes

Let's face it: as much as we might wish otherwise, negotiation doesn't end when we leave the office. From haggling with the cable company over hidden fees to securing a bulk discount on our favorite coffee beans, everyday life is full of opportunities to flex our negotiation muscles.

Why It's Worth Haggling

Sure, it might be easier just to accept the sticker price and move on with your day. But here's the thing: those small savings add up. And more importantly, every successful haggling session is a chance to hone your skills and build confidence.

Think of it like sparring practice for the big fights. The more comfortable you get advocating for yourself in low-stakes situations, the more prepared you'll be when it counts.

Tips for Successful Haggling

1. Do your research

Before you pick up the phone or walk into a negotiation, make sure you know your stuff. What are the market rates for the service or product you're discussing? What kind of discounts or promotions are competitors offering? The more informed you are, the more leverage you have.

2. Ask open-ended questions

Instead of just accepting the first offer, get curious. Ask questions like, "What kind of discounts do you offer for loyal customers?" or "Are there any promotions or bundles I should know about?" You'd be surprised how often these simple queries can lead to unexpected savings.

3. Embrace the power of silence

Once you've made your case or asked your question, resist the urge to fill the silence. Let the other party sit with your request and formulate a response. Often, they'll come back with a better offer just to break the tension.

Real-Life Examples

Let's say you're on the phone with your cable provider, trying to lower your monthly bill. You might start by saying something like, "I've been a loyal customer for three years now, and I'm wondering what kind of discounts you offer for long-term subscribers."

If they come back with a minimal reduction, don't hesitate to push back politely. "I appreciate the offer, but I was hoping for something a bit more substantial. What else can you do to help me stay with your company?"

Or you're at your local coffee shop, hoping to score a bulk discount on your favorite beans. You could say, "I love your coffee and planning to stock up for the month. Do you offer any discounts for larger purchases?"

Even if they don't have a formal bulk pricing program, they might be willing to throw in a few extra bags or a discount code for your loyalty.

The Art of Everyday Haggling

Here's the beauty of haggling in everyday life: the stakes are usually low, but the rewards can be surprisingly high. Every successful negotiation, no matter how small, is a chance to put extra cash in your pocket and a little extra confidence in your step.

So the next time you find yourself facing a negotiation opportunity in the wild, channel your inner ninja. Remember your training, trust your instincts, and don't be afraid to ask for what you want. With a little practice (and a few well-timed silences), you'll be amazed at how quickly haggling becomes second nature.

And who knows? You might look forward to those previously dreaded calls with customer service. After all, when you're a skilled negotiator, every conversation is a chance to flex your muscles and come out on top.

***

How to Get That Raise Without Resorting to Blackmail

Time to talk about the holy grail of workplace negotiations: the raise. It's the conversation that can make even the most seasoned professionals break out in a cold sweat, the one that we rehearse endlessly in the shower but never quite feel ready for when the moment arrives.

But here's the thing: if you're not advocating for your own worth, who will?

Preparing for the Big Ask

Like any high-stakes negotiation, securing a raise requires careful preparation and strategy. Here's how to lay the groundwork:

1. Document your achievements

Start keeping a running list of your accomplishments, big and small. Did you lead a successful project, streamline a clunky process, or score a major client? Write it down, and be as specific as possible. The more concrete evidence you have of your value, the stronger your case will be.

2. Frame it as a win-win

When crafting your pitch, focus on how your raise will benefit the company, not just your bank account. Maybe your increased responsibilities will free up your manager's time, or your new skills will help the team tackle more complex projects. By framing your request as a mutual gain, you increase the chances of a positive outcome.

3. Time it right

Picking the right moment to have the conversation is crucial. Ideally, schedule the discussion after a major win or during your regular performance review. Avoid bringing it up during a stressful crunch time or when your boss is dealing with a crisis.

Handling Pushback Like a Pro

You may still face some resistance even with the most carefully crafted pitch. Here's how to navigate common objections:

1. "It's not in the budget."

Acknowledge the financial constraints, but gently remind them of your value. "I understand budgets are tight, but I believe my contributions have helped us stay on track and increase revenue. Is there any flexibility to revisit my compensation?"

2. "We can't give you a raise right now, but we can offer more responsibility."

This is a tricky one. While taking on more responsibility can lead to a raise down the line, it's important to advocate for your immediate worth. Try something like, "I'm excited to take on new challenges, but I also want to ensure my compensation reflects my current contributions. Could we discuss a phased approach, with a small raise now and a re-evaluation in six months?"

A Real-Life Example

Let's say you're a marketing manager who's been crushing it lately. You've launched a successful campaign, brought in new clients, and generally been a rockstar. You know you deserve a raise, but you're nervous about having the conversation.

You might start by emailing your boss: "Hey Sarah, I'd love to schedule some time to discuss my performance and compensation. I've been taking on additional responsibilities and have some ideas for continuing to drive results for the team. Would you have 30 minutes next week to chat?"

During the meeting, come prepared with your list of accomplishments and a clear ask. "Over the past six months, I've led the launch of our most successful campaign to date, resulting in a 20% increase in leads. I've also taken on the management of our social media channels, freeing up your time to focus on strategy. Given these expanded contributions, I hope to discuss a 10% salary increase."

If your boss pushes back, stay calm and confident. Reiterate your value, and be open to finding a mutually beneficial solution. And if the answer is still no? Don't be afraid to ask what you need to do to earn that raise in the future, and set a timeline for revisiting the conversation.

The Art of Professional Advancement

Negotiating a raise is rarely a one-and-done conversation. It's an ongoing process of demonstrating your worth, advocating for yourself, and being open to feedback and growth.

But here's the beautiful thing: every time you have the conversation, you're not just practicing your negotiation skills but also sending a powerful message about your value and potential. You're showing your boss (and yourself) that you're not content to settle and always striving for more.

So the next time you find yourself daydreaming about that bigger paycheck, remember: you have the tools and the talent to make it happen. And with a little preparation, a lot of confidence, and a few deep breaths, you'll be well on your way to securing the compensation you deserve.

Just promise me one thing: treat yourself to something nice when you land that raise. After all, you've earned it - in more ways than one.

***

Navigating Office Politics with Ninja-Level Skills

Office politics can feel like a corporate game of Twister - uncomfortable, awkward, and you're never quite sure where to put your feet. But fear not, my ninja-in-training! You can turn those political minefields into your personal playground with your newfound negotiation prowess.

Why Office Politics Matter (More Than Your Spreadsheet Skills)

Here's the cold, hard truth: You could be the most brilliant, hardworking professional in the building, but if you can't effectively navigate the complex web of office dynamics, you might as well be invisible.

Mastering the art of relationship-building, forging strategic alliances, and demonstrating interpersonal finesse is like possessing a secret map to the hidden power structure of your organization. And trust me, that map is far more valuable than even the most impressive, color-coded spreadsheets.

In today's collaborative work environments, the true key to career success is your ability to influence, persuade, and build strong relationships across departments and hierarchies. It's not just about what you know; it's about who you know and how you leverage those connections to drive results.

Strategies for Winning the Game (Without Losing Your Soul)

1. Channel Your Inner Sherlock Holmes

   ◦ Map out the informal influence networks (a.k.a., the office gossip chain) to understand who holds the real power

   ◦ Identify the key players, decision-makers, and gatekeepers (hint: they're not always the ones with the fancy titles)

   ◦ Understand what makes each department tick, what motivates them, and what keeps them up at night (besides copious amounts of caffeine and passive-aggressive emails)

2. Build Your Alliance of Awesomeness

   ◦ Cultivate authentic, mutually beneficial relationships across teams and levels (think more "friendly collaboration" than "Machiavellian scheming")

   ◦ Find common ground with colleagues, even if it's just bonding over a shared love of cat memes or commiserating about the office coffee

   ◦ Consistently create win-win situations that make everyone involved look good (because a rising tide lifts all boats or something profound like that)

3. Wield Your Diplomatic Superpowers

- Address conflicts head-on, but always with the tact and grace of a seasoned U.N. ambassador

- Focus on identifying solutions, not assigning blame (save the finger-pointing for the annual chili cook-off fiasco)

- Utilize your active listening and empathy skills to defuse tense situations (and maybe glean some juicy office gossip while you're at it)

Real-World Ninja Move: The Stealth Influencer

Imagine this scenario: You're passionately championing a game-changing project idea, but you're facing more resistance from stakeholders than a toddler faces at bedtime. Rather than charging in with guns blazing, try employing a little ninja-style infiltration:

- Invite key stakeholders to informal coffee chats to better understand their hesitations and concerns

- Thoughtfully tweak your proposal to address their apprehensions (without compromising the core of your brilliant vision)

- Rally support from strategic allies and influencers (you know, the ones with the real behind-the-scenes pull)

- Present a unified, collaborative solution that leaves everyone feeling like a winner (even if you're secretly doing cartwheels of victory in your mind)

The secret is to apply your negotiation skills with a whisper's subtle precision, not a bullhorn's deafening volume. It's less about brazenly dominating the room and more about artfully shaping the conversation and building consensus.

Becoming the Office Politics Grandmaster

Mastering the delicate dance of office politics is an ongoing journey, not a singular destination. It requires continuously honing your emotional intelligence, adaptability, and strategic thinking skills. But with consistent practice and a commitment to wielding your powers for the greater good, you'll soon find yourself effortlessly navigating even the most treacherous corporate landscapes.

So go forth, my savvy negotiator, and conquer the wild world of office politics one strategic coffee chat and carefully orchestrated collaboration at a time! With your growing arsenal of ninja-level people skills, you'll be gracefully ascending the ranks and building your own ladder to success in no time. Just remember to always use your newfound influence for good - and bring a box of gourmet donuts to grease the wheels at your next interdepartmental meeting. Never underestimate the persuasive power of a well-timed pastry delivery.

In the end, mastering office politics is about leveraging your negotiation abilities to build authentic relationships, find common ground, and create mutually beneficial outcomes that propel both you and your organization forward. It's a delicate art but one that pays dividends in both career advancement and personal fulfillment. So embrace the challenge, trust your instincts, and never stop honing your skills - because in the ever-shifting landscape of the modern workplace, the true power lies not in your job title but in your ability to influence, collaborate, and drive meaningful results. And that, my friend, is a lesson worth its weight in office coffee.

Chapter Eight

The 23 Ninja Tricks of Negotiation

My fellow negotiation ninjas, it's time to pull out the big guns. You've mastered the mindset, honed your listening skills, and learned to wield silence like a pro. But what if I told you there were even more tools in your arsenal? Enter: the 23 Ninja Tricks of Negotiation.

Think of this chapter as your secret scroll - a condensed guide to the most powerful, most effective negotiation techniques known to ninja-kind. These tricks will make your counterparts wonder if you've got mind-reading powers, the strategies that will have them saying "yes" before they even realize what's happened.

But here's the thing: with great power comes great responsibility. These tricks aren't about manipulation or deception. They're about understanding human psychology, anticipating needs, and creating win-win outcomes. Used ethically, they'll help you build stronger relationships, close better deals, and navigate even the trickiest negotiation challenges.

So, are you ready to unlock the secrets of the negotiation masters? Grab your metaphorical ninja gear, and let's dive in.

1. **The Aikido Principle**

   - **Description**: Harness your counterpart's energy and momentum in negotiation, much like Aikido, where the practitioner redirects an opponent's force instead of clashing head-on.

   - **Example**: When faced with aggressive pricing demands, rather than outright refusal, use their insistence to discuss value-adds that justify your pricing, such as extended support or additional features.

2. **The Storyteller's Spell**

   - **Description**: Engage your counterpart with compelling stories that illustrate your points, making your message more relatable and memorable.

   - **Example**: Describe a scenario where another client implemented your solution and experienced significant improvements, thus painting a vivid picture of potential success.

3. **The Empathy Jedi**

   - **Description**: Deeply understand and reflect your counterpart's feelings and needs to show genuine comprehension of their situation, which builds rapport.

   - **Example**: If a client expresses concern about implementation challenges, acknowledge their concern by discussing your comprehensive onboarding process tailored to ease them.

4. **The Anchoring Ace**

   - **Description**: Establish the initial figure or stance in the negotiation to set the tone and anchor the subsequent discussions around it.

- **Example**: Propose a higher-than-expected starting salary during a job negotiation to set a high baseline, making the desired salary seem more reasonable.

5. The Reciprocity Ninja

- **Description**: Create a give-and-take dynamic by making strategic concessions or offers, which naturally encourages the other party to reciprocate with something valuable.

- **Example**: Offer an upfront payment discount in exchange for a longer-term contract commitment from the client.

6. The Scarcity Samurai

- **Description**: Emphasize your offer's uniqueness or limited availability to increase its desirability and prompt quicker decision-making.

- **Example**: Mention that the special pricing is exclusive to a select group of clients or available only for a limited time.

7. The Consistency Creed

- **Description**: Leverage your counterpart's desire to appear consistent in their behavior and decisions, referencing their past commitments or statements.

- **Example**: Remind a potential partner of their publicly stated commitment to innovation when proposing your cutting-edge product.

8. The Curiosity Hook

- **Description**: Stimulate interest and engagement by hinting at unique insights or novel outcomes that your negotiation proposal might deliver.

- **Example**: Suggest that your new technology has potential applications they haven't considered, promising to reveal more in further discussions.

9. The Deadlines Dance

- ○ **Description**: Introduce specific time constraints to create urgency, compelling the counterpart to make decisions faster than they might in a more open-ended scenario.

- ○ **Example**: Propose a discount that expires at the end of the business quarter, urging the client to close the deal swiftly to capitalize on the savings.

10. The Mirroring Maverick

- ○ **Description**: Build connection and trust by subtly mirroring your counterpart's body language, tone, and speech patterns, which fosters a subconscious affinity.

- ○ **Example**: If your counterpart speaks thoughtfully and slowly, adopt a similar style to create a more comfortable and congenial negotiation atmosphere.

11. The Labeling Linguist

- ○ **Description**: Identify and articulate the emotions or unstated thoughts your counterpart might be feeling to defuse potential tension and encourage openness.

- ○ **Example**: If a counterpart seems hesitant, you might say, "It seems like there's a concern about the scalability of our solution. What can we explore to address this?"

12. The Calibrated Questioner

- ○ **Description**: Utilize carefully crafted questions to unlock deeper insights into your counterpart's needs and motives, steering the conversation toward mutual understanding.

- **Example**: Instead of a direct question like "Do you agree with our terms?", ask "What aspects of our proposal align well with your objectives, and where do you see room for alignment?"

13. The Acknowledgment Ally

- **Description**: To foster a cooperative environment, show understanding and validation of your counterpart's views or feelings, even if you do not agree with them.

- **Example**: If a client expresses concerns about cost, respond with, "I see your point about budget constraints. Let's explore how we can adjust the scope to meet your financial needs."

14. The Value Detective

- **Description**: Dig deep to discover what your counterpart truly values in a deal, which may not always be obvious or stated, and tailor your proposal accordingly.

- **Example**: If a prospective buyer seems less concerned about price and more about service reliability, focus your proposal on proving the dependability and superior support.

15. The Patience Protector

- **Description**: Exercise patience and avoid rushing the negotiation, giving both parties adequate time to consider the options and build a sustainable agreement.

- **Example**: When a deal is significant, suggest taking a brief pause to reflect or consult with key stakeholders, ensuring all parties feel confident and unhurried in their decision.

16. The Contrast Conjurer

- **Description**: Use contrast to make your proposals more attractive by comparing them against less favorable alternatives, highlighting the benefits and value of your offer.

- **Example**: Outline the potential losses or missed opportunities of sticking with the current vendor versus your solution's comprehensive benefits, painting a stark picture of the advantages.

17. The Social Proof Provider

- **Description**: Leverage the power of social proof by citing examples, testimonials, or case studies from other satisfied customers to validate your claims and enhance your credibility.

- **Example**: Share success stories from well-known clients who have benefited from your service, suggesting that choosing your company is a wise and popular decision.

18. The Objection Opportunist

- **Description**: Treat every objection as an opportunity to understand and address your counterpart's concerns more deeply, using them as springboards for further discussion.

- **Example**: If a potential client objects to a term of service, use it as a chance to discuss their specific needs and customize the agreement, demonstrating flexibility and customer focus.

19. The Concession Closer

- **Description**: Strategically offer concessions that cost you little but have high value to your counterpart, facilitating a sense of progress and goodwill.

- **Example**: Agree to a minor modification in the delivery schedule that doesn't significantly impact your operations but meets the client's urgent needs.

20. The Creativity Catalyst

- **Description**: When negotiations stall, introduce creative alternatives that satisfy both parties' core interests, breaking deadlocks and opening new avenues for agreement.

- **Example**: Propose a partnership or collaboration arrangement instead of a straightforward purchase if a buyer hesitates to commit a large initial investment.

21. The Walkaway Wonder

- **Description**: Know when to walk away from a deal that doesn't meet your minimum requirements, demonstrating confidence in your values and boundaries.

- **Example**: Politely decline a proposal that underestimates the value of your services, reinforcing your business's standards and expectations.

22. The Rapport Ringmaster

- **Description**: Master the art of building rapport by engaging in friendly, genuine conversation that creates a positive atmosphere and fosters mutual trust.

- **Example**: Start meetings with light, personal conversation topics, find common interests, and follow up on previous discussions, showing attentiveness and care.

23. The Persistence Pro

- **Description**: Persistently pursue negotiation goals through multiple interactions, showing resilience and dedication to finding a mutually beneficial outcome.

- **Example**: If initial proposal was declined, come back with modified offer, show flexibility, and maintain a positive, proactive attitude towards achieving an agreement.

Bonus Trick

The Flexibility Facilitator

- **Description**: Show a willingness to adapt and be flexible in negotiations, which can encourage similar flexibility from the other party, leading to more collaborative and innovative solutions.

- **Example**: If a client hesitates to commit to a long-term contract, propose a shorter trial period with the option to extend. This demonstrates your confidence in your service's value and your adaptability to client needs, which can reduce their apprehension and facilitate a quicker decision.

And there you have it - your complete ninja toolkit. But remember, these tricks are just the beginning. Knowing when and how to use them, as well as how to change them to fit your needs, is what gives them their real power.

As you go forth and negotiate, keep this in mind: the ultimate goal isn't just to "win", but to create lasting, mutually beneficial agreements. Use these tricks wisely, and always balance assertiveness with empathy.

Negotiation, like ninja mastery, is a lifelong journey. Each interaction is a chance to learn, grow, and hone your skills. So keep practicing, keep refining your technique, and most importantly, keep collaborating.

Because in the end, the greatest negotiation trick of all is the ability to turn adversaries into allies, challenges into opportunities, and conflicts into creative solutions.

So go forth, my ninja apprentice, and negotiate with skill, integrity, and the unwavering belief that the best deal is one where everyone wins.

The negotiation world is yours to conquer - one carefully crafted conversation at a time.

Chapter Nine

Putting It All Together: Real-World Case Studies

The theory is great, but the practice is where the magic happens. In this chapter, you'll step into the shoes of a negotiation ninja and see how the techniques you've learned play out in real-world scenarios. Plus, you'll discover how even the most experienced ninjas learn from their mistakes—and how you can keep refining your own skills.

Analyzing Successful Negotiations (And Dissecting What Made Them Work)

Let's dive into some juicy real-world examples and break down what made these negotiations successful.

Example 1: The Multi-Million Dollar Merger

Picture this: two tech giants on the brink of a merger. Tensions and stakes are high, and there's enough coffee in the room to fuel a small country.

The key players? A seasoned CEO with a knack for active listening and a CFO who's mastered the art of timing.

As the negotiations heated up, the CEO deployed a classic "Empathy Jedi" move. She built trust and rapport by mirroring the other party's concerns and validating their perspective. This opened the door for her CFO to swoop in with a perfectly-timed "Scarcity Samurai" play, emphasizing their company's unique value.

The result? A mega-merger that left both parties feeling like winners.

The Lesson: Active listening and strategic timing can be the difference between a deal that sinks and one that soars.

Example 2: The Family Vacation Showdown

Negotiation isn't just for the boardroom. Take the classic family vacation debate: beach or mountains? Relaxation or adventure? Dad's wallet or Mom's sanity?

So, in this situation, the teenage daughter—let's just say she's The Negotiation Prodigy—totally came to the rescue. She kicked things off with a "Acknowledgment Ally" vibe, making sure to validate each family member's vacation vision. So, she asked some "Calibrated Questions" to get to the heart of what everyone really wanted: Dad was looking to unplug, Mom was all about that quality family time, and little brother just wanted to make a a splash.

With this info in hand, our genius suggested a beach getaway with a fun twist: a cozy cabin rental that boasts ocean views, family-friendly hikes, and a private pool perfect for cannonball contests.

The Lesson: Understanding each party's underlying needs is the key to crafting a win-win solution. Also, cannonballs are non-negotiable.

✦✦✦

Learning from Common Pitfalls and Mistakes Because Even the Best Ninjas Slip Up Sometimes

Even the most seasoned negotiators can fall prey to common pitfalls. Let's explore some real-life missteps and extract some wisdom from the wreckage.

- **The Overtalker**: We've all been there. We're so excited to make our case that we steamroll the conversation. One ambitious entrepreneur learned this the hard way when pitching his startup to investors. He was so focused on his own script that he missed critical cues from the VCs. The result? A polite "thanks, but no thanks."

The Lesson: Listen more than you speak. Your counterpart's reactions can be more valuable than your own words.

- **The Over-Promiser**: In an effort to close the deal, it's tempting to make promises you can't keep. A freelance designer found herself in hot water when she guaranteed a two-day turnaround on a complex project. When the deadline came and went, her client's trust (and future business) went out the window.

The Lesson: Underpromise and overdeliver. It's better to exceed realistic expectations than to fall short of inflated ones.

- **The Under-Preparer**: Winging it may work for jazzy improv nights, but it's a recipe for disaster in negotiations. Take the case of the sales rep who showed up to a big client meeting sans research. When the client started grilling him on industry trends, he was left fumbling for answers. Needless to say, the deal was dead on arrival.

The Lesson: Do your homework. The more you know about your counterpart and the context, the more prepared you'll be to adapt on the fly.

So, how do you recover when things go south? First, take a deep breath (and maybe a swig of that negotiation juice - aka, extra-strong coffee). Then:

1. **Acknowledge the misstep.** A little humility goes a long way in repairing trust.

2. **Reframe the conversation.** Steer the dialogue back to shared goals and positive solutions.

3. **Propose a path forward.** Come prepared with ideas to get the negotiation back on track.

Remember, mistakes are just learning opportunities in disguise. Embrace them, extract the lessons, and continue honing your ninja skills.

***

How to Be a Chameleon in a Business Suit

Different industries, different rules. What flies in Silicon Valley might flop on Wall Street. The key to cross-industry negotiation success? Adaptability.

Let's compare two worlds: tech and healthcare. In tech, the vibe tends to be casual, the pace breakneck, and the focus on innovation. A savvy negotiator in this space might play up their "Creative Catalyst" side, emphasizing out-of-the-box solutions.

Meanwhile, in healthcare, the tone is more formal, the stakes are often life-or-death, and the priority is on patient outcomes. Here, a "Consistency Creed" approach could be key - aligning proposals with the industry's core mission of improving lives.

But what happens when these worlds collide? Imagine a health-tech startup pitching its AI-powered diagnostic tool to a major hospital. The key is to find common ground (in this case, better patient care) while adapting to the hospital's more formal communication style and decision-making processes.

Some tips for nailing industry adaptability:

1. Do your research. Dive deep into industry norms, jargon, and hot-button issues.

2. Tailor your language. Speak your counterpart's lingo, but steer clear of insider-baseball buzzwords that could come off as inauthentic.

3. Prioritize their priorities. Frame your proposal around the most important outcomes to your counterpart's industry.

4. Be a quick study. Listen carefully and adjust your approach on the fly based on your counterpart's cues.

Think of it like being a chameleon in a business suit: blending into the industry environment, but your true negotiation colors still shine through.

***

Continuous Improvement and Skill Refinement Because the Learning Never Stops

Alright, you've studied the strategies, analyzed the case studies, and even nailed a few negotiations of your own. Time to hang up your ninja hat and call it a day, right?

Not so fast, grasshopper. The truth is, that mastering negotiation is a lifelong journey. The best ninjas never stop training, and neither should you.

Every negotiation, whether it's a major success or an epic fail, is an opportunity to learn and grow. The key is to make reflection a habit.

After each negotiation, ask yourself:

- What worked well?

- What could I have done differently?

- What do I want to try next time?

Jot down your thoughts in a trusty negotiation journal (bonus points if it has a sleek ninja cover). As time goes on, you'll notice some patterns emerging - techniques that work well for you, common mistakes you keep making, and spots where you might want to put in a bit more practice.

But don't just rely on self-reflection. Seek out feedback from peers, mentors, and even counterparts. An outside perspective can be illuminating - and humbling. Embrace it all with the mindset of a perpetual student.

Another ninja tip? Keep your skills sharp by practicing on low-stakes scenarios. Negotiate your cable bill, your kid's bedtime, and your partner's choice of movie night flick. The more you flex your negotiation muscles, the stronger they'll become.

Finally, stay curious. Read the latest negotiation research, follow industry thought leaders, and swap war stories with fellow ninjas. The world of negotiation is always evolving, and so should you.

As you continue your negotiation journey, remember this: mastery isn't a destination, it's a never-ending adventure. Embrace the twists and turns, learn from the triumphs and face-palms, and most of all - enjoy the ride.

Because here's the secret: the true joy of being a negotiation ninja isn't just in the deals you close or the conflicts you resolve. It's in the continuous pursuit of excellence, the thrill of pushing past your comfort zone, and the satisfaction of knowing that with each negotiation, you're not just honing your skills - you're evolving into the best version of yourself.

So keep training, keep growing, and keep unleashing your inner ninja. The negotiation world is waiting for you - and it's sure to be one wild, wonderful ride.

The Negotiation Ninja's Creed

In every interaction, an opportunity.

With every challenge, a chance to rise.

For every misstep, a lesson to learn.

And in every negotiation, a ninja is born.

Conclusion

Embrace Your Inner Negotiation Ninja

Well, my friend, you've made it. You've ventured through the twists and turns of this negotiation journey, picked up a few ninja tricks along the way, and hopefully had a laugh or two at my expense. But this isn't the end - it's just the beginning.

You see, mastering the art of negotiation isn't about reaching some elusive finish line. It's about getting up every morning with the confidence, the skills, and the swag to tackle whatever challenges come your way. Whether you're facing down a boardroom of suits, negotiating bedtime with your kids, or simply trying to score an extra scoop of ice cream at the local diner, you've got this.

Let's take a stroll down memory lane and recap the negotiation nuggets of wisdom that'll stick with you long after you close this book:

Ninja Mindset 101

Remember when we talked about channeling your inner Batman? Embracing that unshakeable confidence, keeping your cool under pressure, and always, always trusting your gut? That's the foundation of any good negotiation. But here's the kicker: confidence isn't about puffing out your chest or putting on a mask. It's about the quiet self-assurance that comes from knowing your worth, your boundaries, and your BATNA (best alternative to a negotiated agreement). So before you step into any negotiation, take a deep breath, roll back those shoulders, and remember: you've got the skills, put in the work, and are ready to rock.

Preparation or Bust

You wouldn't run a marathon without training (unless you're a glutton for punishment). So why walk into a negotiation without doing your homework? We've discussed researching your counterpart, anticipating objections, and crafting value propositions that will make them say, "Tell me more." But preparation isn't just about the facts and figures. It's about getting in the right headspace, clarifying your goals, and visualizing success. So before your next big negotiation, take a page from your favorite sports movie and montage it up. Blast that pump-up playlist, do your power poses and mentally rehearse your win. Trust me, it works.

Words Are Your Superpower

Forget invisibility or flight - the real superpower is the ability to persuade with your words. We've covered utilizing "you" language to connect, painting a vivid picture of benefits, and handling objections like a champ. But here's the thing: persuasive language isn't about manipulation. It's about understanding your audience, speaking to their needs, and finding that sweet spot of mutual benefit. It's about building trust, rapport, and relationships that last long after the deal is done. So choose your words wisely, grasshopper.

The Sounds of Silence

Who knew doing nothing could be so powerful? We've talked about embracing the awkward pause, using silence strategically, and knowing when just to zip it and listen. But let's take it a step further. Silence isn't just a negotiation tactic - it's a life skill. In a world of constant noise and chatter, the ability to be still, reflect, and truly hear others is rare and valuable. So next time you tempted to fill the quiet with needless words, take a beat. Breathe. Listen. You might be surprised at what you learn.

From Boardroom to Living Room

Negotiation isn't just for business hotshots. It's a survival skill for everyday life. We've tackled negotiating with your spouse (good luck with that one), haggling with your cable company, and even asking for a raise without resorting to bribery. But the real magic happens when you start seeing every interaction as a chance to practice your skills. Negotiating bedtime with your toddler? Use that labeling technique to acknowledge their feelings. Trying to score a deal on Craigslist? Break out the social proof and scarcity principle. The more you flex your negotiation muscles, the stronger they become.

Your Negotiation Toolbox

And let's not forget the pièce de résistance - your shiny new set of negotiation tools. From the classic "mirroring" and "labeling" to the more advanced "anchoring" and "loss aversion" - you've now got a whole arsenal of techniques to try out in the real world. But a word of caution: with great power comes great responsibility, so use your powers for good. Aim for win-win outcomes. And always, always keep sharpening your skills. There's no such thing as a perfect negotiator - just a lifelong learner with an unquenchable thirst for knowledge and growth.

So, what now? You close this book, bust out your newfound negotiation chops, and take on the world, right? Well, yes and no. Yes, you should put these hard-earned skills to work every chance you get—practice in low-stakes situations. Negotiate with yourself in the mirror. Get comfortable being uncomfortable. But also remember this: mastery is a moving target. There will be hiccups, fumbles, and the occasional face-palm along the way. And that's okay! In fact, it's more than okay - it's essential to your growth.

So here's my challenge to you, my intrepid negotiation ninja: keep learning. Keep pushing yourself out of your comfort zone. Seek out new challenges, new perspectives, and new opportunities to flex your muscles. Read books, listen to podcasts, find a mentor, and teach others what you know. The world of negotiation is vast and ever-evolving - and so are you.

And while you're out there kicking butt and taking names, I've got one last teensy favor to ask. If this book has made a difference in your life - if it's helped you snag a sweeter deal, navigate a tricky conversation, or feel more confident in your skin - pay it forward. Share your story. Write a review. Tell your friends, your colleagues, your book club buddies. Because the more we can spread the gospel of effective negotiation, the better off we'll all be. After all, isn't the whole point of mastering negotiation to create a world with a little less conflict and a little more collaboration?

So here's to you, you brilliant, badass, negotiation ninja. May your bargaining be bold, your agreements abundant, and your guacamole always free of charge. Now get out there and show 'em what you're made of.

And remember, if you ever need a pep talk, a strategy session, or a sympathetic ear - I'm only a page turn away. Okay, more like a re-read away. But you get the point.

Keep shining, keep growing, and keep negotiating like your life depends on it. Because in a way - it does.

Signing off with a fist bump and a wink,

Your faithful negotiation guide

About the author

Check out Julian's author profile on Amazon

www.ingramcontent.com/pod-product-compliance
Lightning Source LLC
Chambersburg PA
CBHW071716210326
41597CB00017B/2507